P9-EDA-199

PARENTING

Principles and Politics
of Parenthood

SIDNEY CORNELIA CALLAHAN

DOUBLEDAY & COMPANY, INC.
GARDEN CITY, NEW YORK
1973

ISBN: 0-385-04553-0
Library of Congress Catalog Card Number 72–175361

To my parents

and my children

Contents

Prologue

Parenting is a process and an idea which provokes universal reactions. Moreover, at the present moment public controversies over the role and rights of parents are everywhere emerging. Questions of parenting cannot help but press home, for each person who participates is an interested party. Everyone has parents, or has had parents, and lived to tell the tale. Other multitudes of people are practicing parents, and when they discuss the issues, they refer to their own lives. Never has there been so much firsthand experience to fuel thought and raise consciousness.

But because the subject of parenthood is so intimate, so serious, many of us defend ourselves against it in various time-honored ways. Laughter and joking about child rearing pervades the current scene. There are a number of hilarious books on the personal experiences of parents, which in witty prose or poetry keep us laughing—and laughing. Family comedies on TV, movies, cartoons, humor magazines—most of the popular media in some way present parent-child relationships as one endless stream of amusing incidents. There even exists a TV show entitled "The Parent Game," played for laughs, with real

(?) parents presenting solutions to parental inquiries. In comedies, of course, everything turns out all right in the end; or if it doesn't, the disasters deepen the joke. We laugh instead of cry.

Another more sophisticated defense denies and rejects all need to think about parenthood. After all, did not Freud say that when you ask the meaning of life, it is a sign of sickness? Isn't it the same when questioning parenthood? Even to think about thinking about parenting is a sign that we're in trouble. Right. Admittedly. That's just the point; we *are* in trouble. We ask questions because we don't know the answers, and the questions cannot be avoided. Decisions which we must make, individually and collectively, demand our thought. External necessity and immutable tradition no longer solve the problems of parenting.

Faced with new choices we cannot avoid, we can believe in believing or opt to think. I believe one can never think too well, especially about murky, threatening, impossibly sprawling questions like parenthood. Just organizing the different areas of inquiry is a challenge. There are few guides for producing an overview of parenting or ferreting out any essential principles in the multitude of disciplines involved. It is one of those subjects where there's unlimited information, little coherence and less wisdom. Too few sources attempt to blend personal parental experience, current theory, and sociocultural observation.

As a practicing parent seeking an intellectual understanding of parenthood, I cannot help but be drawn to a multidimensioned discussion—seeking wholeness and passionate clarity. Selection, however, is as necessary as it is distorting, so I divide the book into six chapters involving quite central questions. I begin by asking who we are as American parents: Are we unique or do we share certain essential experiences of parenting with other cultures before us?

Next I plunge with audacity into the quicksands of value judgments and presume to describe what good parents do. Naturally, I here skim over issues which are developed in the rest of the book. This chapter on good parenting is a compressed synthesis of the research I have done, my own parental experience and a lifetime's observations of parenting. Some people, mostly desperate parents, may read this chapter first. If practicing parents are disappointed at the lack of specific advice, they should read the next chapter dealing with "how to read how-to parent books" and immediately proceed to the guidebooks of experts. Forewarned is forearmed.

In chapter four I struggle with questions invariably avoided by popular parent guides: parental relationships with others outside the parent-child interaction. Since this also brings up the responsibility and rights of parents and children vis-à-vis the larger community, I call this chapter parent-child politics. Confronting the hard questions of rights, power, restraints and the law, I am finally forced into the most difficult questions of all. Chapter five deals with the incredibly difficult but deceptive question: Are parents born or made? This discussion which takes a developmental approach, ranges through the nature-nurture question and prepares the ground for the final chapter on future parenting. What will parents be in the future? Naturally this discussion is loaded with more value judgments in the fashion of futurology, also ending, I am afraid, with a pious hope. The Epilogue brings me back to the concrete experiential present with all the inevitable regrets for failing to carry out my original vision of the book. But then to effectively bring about a progress from conception to maturity is the essence of the subject.

Who Are We as American Parents?

Parents in America are under enough pressure of varying kinds so that they often find themselves uncertain and confused. Cases of parental panic are not unknown and epidemics of severe parental anxiety can sweep through a neighborhood, or even the whole society. Parental anxiety can arise in the face of a clear and present physical danger such as the outbreak of disease, but cases of youthful drug abuse or sexual promiscuity can arouse even more worry. The latter problems may seem but the tip of an iceberg; while submerged lie more chilling questions. Is the whole society falling apart? Or to take the opposite tack, which is just as worrisome, are we coming into an era of new consciousness which demands radical change in parent-child relationships?

Personally, I foresee neither disintegration and collapse nor the imminence of a golden age. Prophets of Consciousness III seem as mistaken as the followers of Chicken Little, always sure that the sky is falling. But I do think American parents are in for a time of self-consciousness and re-examination of goals which we have come to call consciousness-raising. Inside the family and out, there has been enough change in the social scene to warrant a major rethinking of what parenting is all about. Old slogans or reversions to an 1890s approach won't suffice. What are we doing when we have children and rear them? What are we trying to do? There is enough confusion over the goals of parenting in our pluralistic society to create tension in the schools, the courts, and between experts and various professionals.

Parents who are caught in the cultural ferment have to make more and more hard decisions. Naturally, responsible parents worry. But the nature of parenthood in America almost precludes co-operative efforts to come to creative new solutions. Often parents are constrained from even talking about their problems. In the beginning of the drug epidemic in our suburban town, the parents suffered deeply, but mostly alone. Each family without contacts or the support of others considered their problem an individual parental failure. As one father said, looking back on those years of helpless agony: "The kids were united, but the parents couldn't get together. None of us were able to break the isolating barriers and help each other." Only now, five years later, after drug-related deaths, mental breakdowns, police persecution, academic careers ruined, and other painful things, have the parents and other adults in the community mobilized in a co-operative effort to fight drug abuse among the young. Parents are no longer alone on one issue in one small community, but drug use is only one issue among many.

Parents want to know whether there are any basic principles of parenting which can help them understand and be prepared for the multitude of issues which arise. Are there any essential patterns to the parent-child relationship? And what about the parent's relationship to others? Many a harassed parent cannot help but ask: Has child rearing ever been so difficult before, or is our twentieth-century American experience of parenting unique? In answer, I would maintain that there is a deep structure to all parenting and a universal patterning of the process. But at the same time there is also much diversity in parent-child relationships arising from the variety of human cultures and particular historical processes. Thus, American parents have much in common with all parents everywhere, share more characteristics with others in the stream of Western tradition, and finally are most influenced by the specific American experience. Our own American tradition and environment powerfully shape our parental expectancies and parental practice. Facing present-day confusion and the prospect of future change, we can take a case history of American parenthood and try to determine what we have in common with all parents everywhere and what is particularly our own.

The situation is made more difficult because as Jules Henry the anthropologist says: "In no culture is a child merely a child, but someone representing the cultural values."[1] The infant who comes new into the world presents a screen upon which the culture's idea about the nature and destiny of man is projected. Perhaps the dynamics of this would be much like a collective response to an ink blot test—the ambiguous stimulus of the infant gets interpreted with very basic beliefs about human beings in general. But when you add parenting to the test and make it a moving picture to be interpreted, you get even more revelations of a culture. In the parent-child process there is at least a face-to-face interaction over an extended time span. Therefore, basic cultural attitudes and assumptions involving time, achievement, values, and personal interrelationships become important. Inevitably interpretations of parenting reveal a culture's attitudes to power, sex, aggression, and other priorities.

Two prominent students of the interrelationships of child rearing and culture, John M. Whiting and Irvin Child, main-

[1] Jules Henry, *Pathways to Madness* (New York: Random House, 1971), p. 336.

tain that it is always necessary to remember "the dependence of child training upon the maintenance systems of society."[2] Those who would intervene to change a culture by changing child-rearing practices alone are forewarned. "Advice about child training in our society has too often been promulgated without adequate attention to this dependence, as though child-training practices were an entirely independent element which could be altered at will. The cultural context needs to be examined carefully both to judge the probable difficulty of effecting a change and to judge what other effects a change might have in addition to the effects that are intended."[3] In other words, parents or others cannot simply import Samoan adolescent behavior or Russian nurseries to the United States without being beset by unforeseen consequences and complications.

Parent-child relationships exist embedded in distinct cultures in which different elements or systems are integrated and function as parts of a whole. The pioneer anthropologist Ruth Benedict spoke of these cultural wholes as patterns of culture or configurations. She affirmed that since "Culture is not a biologically transmitted complex," and as it is transmitted over time, the special selections made by a particular culture are maintained: "It is in cultural life as it is in speech; selection is the prime necessity."[4] I am not so sure that in our present shrinking world differing cultural patterns or "configurations" can long continue to hold together with much inner consistency. Still it can be said that distinct cultural configurations continue to exist. America is still different from Afghanistan, even if the sameness of jetports in the world can lead to the prediction that the spread of technology and industrialization might signal the end of all differences.

[2] John W. M. Whiting and Irvin L. Child, *Child Training and Personality* (New Haven: Yale University Press, 1953), p. 321.
[3] *Ibid.*
[4] Ruth Benedict, *Patterns of Culture* (Boston: Houghton Mifflin Co., 1934), p. 23.

But what of universals and cross-cultural constancies in child rearing? Parenting may be the universal way a culture reproduces itself from one generation to the next, but what else is the same? Again we can turn to John Whiting and Irvin Child and their study, *Child Training and Personality*. Building on the work of many other students of human behavior and culture, Whiting and Child tried to create a method to analyze the interaction of child rearing and culture. They used anthropological observations of seventy-five different societies, setting up as universal categories five systems of behavior—oral, anal, sexual, dependence, and aggression. They assumed these systems would be universal, since the first three are motivated by the primary or innate drives of hunger, elimination, and sex, and dependency is necessary for infant survival. Aggression, too, seems a universally occurring experience in childhood and adult human life—whether it arises from frustration or is biologically innate. As Whiting and Child explain their schemata, they say:

> It appears that in every society children must be weaned from breast to bottle and taught to eat food in an appropriate manner; that in every society children must be taught to defecate at the proper time and the proper place; that in every society children must be taught the rules of sexual propriety; that in every society children must be taught to be self-reliant and responsible; and that in every society children must be taught to curb their aggressive impulses and express them only when it is considered appropriate or tolerable by the rules of the society.[5]

This could be a statement of the rules about rules that parents, including American parents, have to follow when raising children.

[5] Whiting and Child, *op. cit.*, p. 46.

But in almost every society, there is also an initial learning considered appropriate for a child, followed by a time of socialization when the child's way must give way to behavior appropriate for older children and adults. In these transitions differences appear in the timetables and intensity with which child training is done. As Whiting and Child state it, "Societies differ from one another in the degree to which children are indulged during the initial period and in the severity of the discipline imposed during the socialization period."[6] Another variable is found in who does the training and how. Societies (and also classes and ethnic groups within a complex society like ours) differ widely in the methods which are considered appropriate to child rearing. Underlying these differences, however, are the basic similarities in the necessary "nurturant socialization"[7] of all cultures, induced by the human condition. The deep structures of all parenting let Whiting and Child conclude that "Child training the world over is in certain important respects identical. . . . Parents everywhere have similar problems to solve in bringing up their children."[8]

There may be even more cross-cultural constancies in parenting, more rules about rules, than Whiting and Child enumerate. They are focusing upon the parenting and socialization of infants and small children and do not investigate the relationship of parents and their older or adult children. The end of life might have its own dependency patterns of parents and children (this time with parents dependent upon children). Death and dying is as universal as birth and socialization. Also, in the middle of life there may be cross-cultural constancies in parent-child relationships having to do with launching chil-

6 *Ibid.*, p. 47.
7 Ira L. Reiss, "The Universality of the Family: A Conceptual Analysis," *Journal of Marriage and the Family,* 27 (November 1965), pp. 443–53.
8 Whiting and Child, *op. cit.*, p. 63. *cf.* also, Bronislaw Malinowski, "Parenthood, The Basis of Social Structure," *The Family: Its Structure and Functions* (Rose Laub Coser, ed. New York: St. Martin's Press, 1964), pp. 3–18.

dren as independent adults in the society (puberty rites, etc.)
and the transmission of property and status from parents to
children. Our problems with our adolescents of thirteen to
twenty-four may reflect general launching difficulties which occur much earlier and more briefly in other groups. Parents
maintain a culture in more ways than the initial reproduction
and socialization of children.

Much of the study of older parent-child relationships has
been part of studies of the whole family as an institution in
society.[9] In primitive cultures, kinship and family may be the
primary organizing principle of the community. As societies become more complex, so does the problem of the interaction
of family and society. When a culture and society gets to the
point where there is a political organization, or religious organization, or other economic and social extrafamily systems
within the society, are there then any constant relationships
which hold?

One theory has it that when times are good, and the society's
political organization is highly developed, the family recedes
in influence. As one French legal historian of family ties notes:

In fact, the family is the first refuge in which the threatened
individual takes shelter when the authority of the State
weakens. But as soon as political institutions afford him adequate guarantees, he shakes off the constraint of the family
and the ties of blood are loosened. The history of lineage
is a succession of contractions and relaxations whose rhythm
follows the modifications of the political order.[10]

[9] Anthropology and sociology both take the family as their province.
Three classics which give an overview of the work done are Talcott Parsons
and Robert F. Bales, *Family, Socialization and Interaction Process* (Glencoe:
The Free Press, 1955); N. W. Bell and E. F. Vogel, eds., *A Modern
Introduction to the Family* (Glencoe: The Free Press, 1960); William
Goode, *World Revolution and Family Patterns* (New York: Macmillan,
1963).
[10] G. Dubuy, quoted in Philippe Ariès, *Centuries of Childhood: A Social
History* (New York: Vintage Books, 1962), p. 355.

Luigi Barzini and other analysts of the Italian family would say the same about the interaction of politics and family in Italian history.[11] Perhaps in Western European history the family turns in upon itself and maintains ties with relatives during bad times. We need more histories of the family as an institution and ideal, with special emphasis upon the parent's function and role.[12]

Of course, one's very definition of "family" can differ from context to context. There is the "family of origin" from which one comes. There is the "family of procreation" in which one is a parent. There is the "extended family" in which other kinfolk either reside with you or live close enough to be important. Then there is the modern "nuclear family," or "conjugal family," which consists mainly of parents and their immediate children. Oddly enough, we are producing new-style nuclear families in America when multiple marriages and multiple offspring create new mixed households and ambiguous kinship. ("Meet my stepmother's stepchild from her first marriage," etc.) Obviously, different cultures have sanctioned different forms of family organization and there are varieties and divergences within different historical periods as well.

But what are the correlations between psychological relationships and variations in family form? I think R. D. Laing is correct when he stresses the importance of the "family" as a psychic fantasy structure each member has internalized.[13] Family members do share a coinherence, or sense of belonging, to their own family which deeply affects their lives. Is this internalized sense of belonging of parents and children always more intense (both positively and negatively) when they are more isolated together in a nuclear family? What is the effect

[11] Luigi Barzini, *The Italians* (New York: Bantam Books, 1964), pp. 198–222.
[12] Ariès' pioneering work on the changing concepts of the family in France should be a model for investigating changing parental consciousness.
[13] R. D. Laing, *The Politics of the Family and Other Essays* (New York: Vintage Books, 1969), pp. 4–6.

of the presence of other relatives in the household? In the neighborhood? Surely the cultural expectancies, economic situation, and values of the persons involved are tremendously important in answering such difficult questions. Unfortunately, the complexity and variability of all the factors involved in family dynamics are just beginning to be investigated.[14] Many varieties of parental experience may emerge from such historical and cross-cultural psychological studies.

But here, let us concentrate on parenting in our own American culture. Granted, American culture is hybrid, pluralistic, and incredibly complicated, but we know it most thoroughly as participating observers. Even as I write from a white, middle-class, feminine, northern-European, southern-U.S. tradition, I have more in common with most present Americans than I do with twentieth-century Javanese culture or a ninth-century Chinese society. As a Canadian missionary once remarked of his difficulties among the Indians of Peru, "I found out my basic religion was Saskatchewan." His North American Canadian conditioning was formative; he had already been given his internal maps of the world and learned all the basic rules about rules.[15] The assumptions about life you don't even know you make are the strongest and contribute most to "culture shock." The majority of Americans cannot help but share in a common set of expectancies and assumptions, especially when it comes to parenthood.

We could say that most American parents are heir to the highly pressured parental experiences of an immigrant people. Coming to a new world increases all the constant problems of parenthood. If one immigrates with children, all the difficulties of protection and providing a livelihood are increased by the

[14] David H. Olson, "Marital and Family Therapy: Integrative Review and Critique," *Journal of Marriage and the Family*, 32 (November 1970), pp. 501–38.
[15] Laing, *op. cit.*, "Rules and Metarules," pp. 103–16.

insecurity and vulnerability of parents facing the unknown. A nomadic people may so organize themselves that travel is a way of life, but when settlers move to a new land, the transition is difficult and full of stress. Energy is being expended on survival and adjustment and the parent-child relationship may be an added burden. (Even today, accidents are more likely to occur to young children during a family move.)

Anxiety over meeting new challenges is also the immigrants' lot. There is a great deal of psychic stress added to physical turmoil. Exile has always been a punishment and homesickness a common malady. The mental strain of adapting to a new country can create negative pressures on family life. Anxiety, uncertainty, fatigue, and frustration on the part of parents are always felt by children. Normal worries are intensified when stability and security are threatened. When one looks at the death rates of the early struggling colonists in this harsh land, one can imagine the stress and strain that American parents felt from the beginning.

If the earliest American immigrants had nature and hostile natives to contend with, later immigrants had wage slavery, slums, and prejudice to produce insecurity and stress.[16] Being despised as foreigners or riffraff was as bitter an experience as those first devastating winters in the Plymouth colony and Jamestown. An inability to cope with a strange culture makes the protective and socialization functions of parenthood most precarious. Many, many American parents have had to bear the stress of being newcomers.

Even after immigration to America (voluntary or enslaved) families and individuals would follow a pattern of internal immigration. American history is a progression of western frontier movements, internal farm-to-city migrations or present-day movements to different regions in the country. Keep going.

[16] Oscar Handlin, *The Uprooted* (New York: Grosset & Dunlap, 1951).

A more restless, mobile people would be hard to find. And Americans, in contrast to gypsies, Beduoins, and other migrating people, do not migrate in kinship groups. There have been many extended family and religious sect migrations in American history, and one's kin may follow later, but the dominant pattern has been the individual nuclear family moving to follow employment or the individual youth striking out on his own. Therefore, many parents in America have been, and are still, isolated from the support of a secure, stable circle of friends, relations, and fellow believers, with an established way of life.

Today, one recurring argument about American family life turns on whether kin beyond the immediate family are important or not.[17] Do kin help each other as extended families in Europe do? Are American nuclear families really as isolated as has been asserted? Apparently, kin are more important psychologically and economically than has been recognized, but on a day-to-day basis most American families do not seem able to expect much help from outside the immediate conjugal family. Competition, isolation, mobility, privacy, innovation have been values more dominant than co-operation, stability, and group traditions. An American family can be very much alone.

The psychic price of moving and change of living environment may still be unrecognized. In an article entitled "Moving and Depression in Women"[18] Myrna M. Weissman and Eugene S. Paykel describe the strains on modern family life that moving brings. No class is exempt here, because upper-middle-class families, "the new migrant workers," move to pursue career goals and are subject to as much stress as working-class or poor families suffering forced dislocation by urban removal. The general belief that "Americans have adapted to the geo-

17 Burt N. Adams, "Isolation, Function, and Beyond: American Kinship in the 1960's," *Journal of Marriage and the Family*, 32 (November 1970), pp. 575–97.
18 Myrna M. Weissman and Eugene S. Paykel, "Moving and Depression in Women," *Society* (July–August 1972), pp. 24–28.

graphical mobility of contemporary life with relative ease and little anxiety"[19] may not be true. Familiar ties, social support, and community interaction are disrupted by moving, even when the move is voluntary and, like a lot of moves up the ladder, supposedly desirable.

Women suffer the most from moving, since the husband generally initiates a move to further his career and women are left to reconstruct domestic and social life. Consider the advertisement which shows the woman in tears at the thought of her husband's promotion and move. Women may be frustrated in their own career developments by moving, or just be socially lonely. However, in studies of male and female depressed patients a recent geographical move was frequently a factor. "But," as Weissman and Paykel say, "social pressures inhibit personal acceptance of this stress, and difficulties in coping with the problems of moving come to be regarded as personal inadequacies and failures."[20] It is so built-in to America that one ought to be able to move on and do new things that we don't even recognize it as involving stress. Yet, "Moving often places inordinate demands on the individual to adapt and raises continued challenges to his identity. While many people move each year and experience no problems or only transient ones, there are a substantial number of persons who do experience incapacitating suffering."[21] And these authors don't even go into the extra stress moving imposes upon the parental role. The question inevitably arises again, why *do* we move so much?

Even if one grows up in a stable enclave of settled people and established ways, the American dream of mobility, adventure, and new frontiers can successfully siphon off the young people. Leaving home is a profound part of the American experience. The high value of independence and individualism is

[19] *Ibid.*, p. 24.
[20] *Ibid.*
[21] *Ibid.*, p. 28.

built-in to American cultural assumptions. Mobile independence has remained a primary value for this country, partly because of our incredible wealth, size, and natural resources. The beautiful rich land lay before the new settlers, waiting to be cultivated. The new frontier which was always there set the special tone of the whole culture. Our national optimism was based upon natural opportunity.

If it wasn't land, it was untapped trade, mining, oil, lumber, manufacturing, and so on. Success followed upon innovation for those daring to change. Leaving home and making personal and social progress were all of a piece. The old ways, of either grandparents, parents, or the old country, had to be discarded in the name of progress and success. From the very beginning, "The fathers, fumbling through the forests for paths they did not recognize, lost the ability to assure their sons of the way."[22] Change has been so much a part of American culture that the generation gap (or loss of authority to lead) was a perennial problem. Geography was godmother (and a generous fairy godmother at that) to America's mobility, long before innovative technology took over.

Since we have enumerated the stress and strains of immigration and mobility upon parenting, it is only fair to enumerate the positive parental conditions in America. The same emphasis upon progress and change which removed parental supports encouraged parental hope. With some form of frontier always there, parents never had to resign themselves to despair; their children could always rise above their own hardships. Hope for their children brought the immigrants to the new world and filled the frontiers. Coming from circumscribed caste and class-bound old societies where the land and the wealth had already been cornered, parents could aspire for themselves and their children in a society of new "self-made"

[22] Oscar Handlin and Mary F. Handlin, *Facing Life: Youth and the Family in American History* (Boston: Little, Brown & Co., 1971), p. 16.

men. The stress, the strain, the insecurity, the sacrifices of new settlers were not in vain. Often hopes were more than fulfilled in America, the land of opportunity (always excepting the fate of Indians, Blacks and Mexican-Americans).

From a child's point of view the stress and strains of American family life could also have benefits. Intolerable parents and kinfolk did not have to be borne forever. Submission, obedience, conformity, and traditionalism could be left behind. A "Declaration of Independence" could be successful. Youth in a new country could try new things—from fashion to occupations to family lifestyles. Children were influenced by their parents' optimistic hopes as well as by their anxieties and uncertainties. Part of America's success and wealth has come from a trust in trying new ways and a belief in improvement. Optimism and idealistic hope, the ability to break set, may be the preconditions for creativity. Even the insecurity and challenges of youthful independence may encourage creativity. The Enlightenment belief in future progress was entrenched in America because, by and large, for most of the people the environment confirmed optimism.

Stress, strains, change, individualism, and optimism still mark the culture American parents inhabit and reproduce. The ideology and experience of American parenthood has been shaped in these special directions.[23] Old World folk culture, religion, literature, and intellectual fashions have been an influence in American parent-child politics in a special American way. The New World did not simply reproduce or transmit Old World culture, despite names such as New England or New York. Enough has already been written on the distinctive character of American culture and literature, but a few more words are in order when attempting to understand American parenthood.

First, it is interesting to note that both fairy stories and

[23] Robert R. Sears, Eleanor Maccoby, and Harry Levin, *Patterns of Child Rearing* (Evanston, Ill.: Row, Peterson & Co., 1957).

Greek classical mythology were never as formative for American culture as they were in Europe. The pessimism and tragedy of Greek culture may have touched our educated elite, but did not influence the masses. Fate and ideas of unredeemed suffering make no sense to a people who have never known poverty, the ravages of war, or defeat. In America neither Prometheus nor Pandora has ever been punished for their defiance of parental authorities. Incestual family murders, blood feuds, and pursuing Furies may not take on reality unless all escapes (all frontiers) are closed and available resources scarce. External conflicts with raw nature have kept America from those enclosed, introspective depths of hatred and hopelessness. Parents and children could turn aggression outward. True, we have O'Neill's plays and Faulkner's novels, but these are more recent and come from regions long settled with people living in untypically stagnant social situations. A trapped, conflicted vision of life has never gained ascendancy in America. (Of course we have also paid a price for our lack of tragedy.) The Greek heritage America nurtures has been that of light, order, rationality, analysis, and mastery of nature. We select for sun, education, and the Olympic games, while leaving the Eleusinian mysteries, Oedipus, and fate to Europe. The inevitability of family conflicts, fatalism, and ambivalence is very foreign.

In the same way, European fairy stories are selected as they enter American culture. The more grim tales in Grimm's fairy stories remain untold. We opt for Cinderella and Boots who triumph in the end over obstacles and elder siblings. The Little Mermaid, model of masochism and unavoidable conflict, is enshrined in a statue in European waters. Even when we tell of Hansel and Gretel, it's the Wicked Witch who gets the attention, not the parents who first abandoned the children to the forest. Surely fairy stories were always ways for parental hostility to be recognized and vented upon, and by, children. A study of parenthood in folk literature should be pursued. The struggling, good loving parents are either helpless or far out-numbered by the punitive, rejecting fathers and torturing step-mothers. Sometimes the child is mutilated or incarcerated when he does not obey his parents. Favoritism and scapegoating are rife, too, of course. Fantasy in fairy tales has a very unsavory side, even before you begin on Freudian analyses of uncon-scious sexual symbolism. Whether or not enchanted frogs sym-bolize sexual organs, the parents behave with unrelieved malice.

Of course, one could explain America's weak adherence to fairy stories with the cynical observation that Americans have always had Indians and Blacks upon which to project folk fan-tasies. Children could be frightened with Indian massacres rather than demons or fairy retribution. Indians and Blacks could supply material for the strange, the weird, and the per-verse. Heroes could struggle with nature, wild Indians, or renegade villains. The myth of cowboy and Indian and good and evil on the frontier absorbed imaginative energies and left little room for kings, princesses, trolls, fairies, and other deni-zens of ancient lands. In American folklore, ambiguity and ambivalence are in short supply; suffering is soon over and success more likely—for the morally virtuous.

The special American selectivity operating on traditional European culture is an optimistic faith that virtue may be re-warded in this life. There exists a resolution to each dilemma (perhaps involving a new technique), a way to triumph over evil, and with enough effort the good win out over all odds. How deeply this has sunk into our collective bones! My own high school motto (the subject of salacious humor) was "I shall find a way or make one." How typical of America, the home of true grit and progress. Condorcet, that revolutionary optimist, believed all the way to the guillotine in the inevitable future progress of man. His was an American spirit. Indeed all Amer-ica was influenced by utopian dreams. Perfectibility was possi-ble with enough rational planning, hard work, and moral virtue. Parents were, of course, a crucial link in ideologies of progress; they were implementors of the faith—be it secular or religious.

This brings us to perhaps the most influential factor in shaping American culture, the Judaeo-Christian faith. Many of the immigrants came to America for religious freedom, and those that did not were soon subject to the religious and moral atmosphere of the land. Frequent great revivals and awakenings swept the country (one may even now be in progress) and tried to convert those who remained unchurched. What can one say of this vast seething stew of religious thought and feeling? It was generally Protestant, since Catholics, Jews, and others were a minority at the beginning, and a minority influenced by Americanism at that. Moreover, most of the religious groups and sects represented dissent and separatism from an established church.[24] That did not keep strict theocracies from flourishing here and there, but mostly the thrust of American Christianity was toward a new, reforming version of the Gospel. The freedom and liberty of the freeborn sons of God was a strong persisting theme. Note that the central image is a parent-child relationship with God as Father. Theological concepts of the priesthood of all believers and the inherence of the Spirit within every man were also conducive to democracy. Those who did not adhere to a sect directly in the Anabaptist tradition, proclaiming freedom and equality, could get their belief in the spirit of Man, with a capital M, indirectly from the thinkers of the Enlightenment. Together with all who felt they were a saved remnant, or precursors of the perfectibility of mankind, such believers insured a general optimism in and out of American religion.

Firm doctrines of original sin never seemed to be able to quell American optimism. Even in New England the devil

[24] H. Richard Niebuhr, *The Kingdom of God in America* (New York: Harper Bros., 1959).

could never triumph over the consciousness of the efficacy of Christ's saving grace. As usual in arguments between those who emphasized faith and those who emphasized works, the believers in faith worked like hell. Apparently, proving one's faith and living out predestination takes will power, strict character formation, and an uncompromising work ethic. All of which virtues have to be given to children early. In my ancestral Alabama town there was once a schism among Baptists (thus fares pluralism in some parts). The split arose over an argument about predestination, and the two factions were nicknamed "the help-its" and "the can't-help-its." Needless to say, "the can't-help-its" always tried harder.

When fervent work habits produce worldly success, that, too, is a sign of grace and divine favor. In an abundant land which has never had plague, famine, or conquest, it seems easy to know that God sheds his grace on thee. No wonder that Christianity in America was always subject to fits of perfectionism. Perfectibility here on earth was the characteristic American heresy—Pelagianism resurrected. The "hundred possibly thousands of Utopian communities,"[25] which have been founded in America from 1680 on, took religious inspiration from the idea that the Kingdom of Heaven was not only within each man, or not only at the end of time in the second coming of Christ, but also could be lived fully here on earth. If man could rearrange the social environment on the proper principles, then Utopia would no longer be "Nowhere" but Somewhere, U.S.A. While utopian communities were as diverse as Oneida and Brook Farm, and most eventually floundered, they were microcosms of general American millenarianism. The utopian community was an intense concrete example of New World optimism with its roots in the Enlightenment and Christian

[25] Rosabeth Moss Kanter, *Commitment and Community: Communes and Utopias in Sociological Perspective* (Cambridge: Harvard University Press, 1972), p. 3.

optimism. A student of American communes can say that, like God, communes were a refuge and a hope for "the primary utopian idea is human perfectibility."[26]

Naturally these currents in America affected the American ideology of parenthood. Indeed, one can trace a process in which home and family became an everyman's Utopia. Historians have traced the rise in the nineteenth century of the cult of home and family (with parents as its priests) to spreading disillusionment with an increasingly industrialized nation. The increase of population, complexity, disorder, urbanization, and cynical materialism made the early republican dream less viable. Americans turned away from the ideal of citizenship or church membership in the elect and began a retreat to home sweet home. The New World did not seem so new and the precariousness of life, especially city life, now began to seem more dangerous. Home and family became a shelter and the recipient of the energy that before had gone into church and commonwealth.

Parents tried to reproduce the family farm ideal in miniature as they fled the city. The move to the suburbs was begun in a nostalgic effort to recapture an older, simpler, more wholesome, purer form of life. The fact that a member of the family (the father) had to go to the city to earn a living was ignored and compensated for in the sylvan retreat of home. The home, like Utopia, became an enclave where perfect love, freedom, leisure, and goodness could reign.

Kirk Jeffrey details this movement in his article on "The Family as Utopian Retreat from the City: The Nineteenth-Century Contribution."[27] He shows the growth of the ideal of the "Edenic home" with extravagant expectations "that domestic life ought to be perfect and could be made so. Through careful design of the home as a physical entity, and equally

26 *Ibid.*, p. 33.
27 Kirk Jeffrey, "The Family as Utopian Retreat from the City," *Soundings*, 55 (Spring 1972), pp. 21–41.

painstaking attention to the human relationships which would develop within it, the family could actually become a heaven on earth."[28] So began present middle-class patterns, expectations, and consequent "strain, tension and guilt."[29] Jeffrey maintains that in these homes individualism and libertarian ideals were nurtured, but this cult of privatism was not viewed as inconsistent with the good of the group or the larger social order. The Edenic home would send forth moral individuals who would redeem and reform society, although they were reared apart from society's corrupting influence. No conflict was seen between the interests of the individual, the family, or the country. What's good for the family member is good for the country.

Just as immigrants had left an old world, just as commune members left the larger society, so the ideal American home was a separate parental retreat from the uncontrolled disordered world. Here there seems to be a relationship between family and larger society, so that when times are bad or unpleasant, families turn in on themselves and withdraw. They reconstruct a social reality which is coherent and comforting. The difference, of course, between American patterns and European precedents is the frequent absence of an extended kinship network or stable neighborhood to alleviate the family's daily isolation in its retreat. An uprooted pseudoagrarian suburban society dedicated to perfection is different from real, rooted country living.

New kinds of stress, arising from the mix of withdrawal, individualism, innovation, and hope, loaded down the parental process. Idealism, optimism, and utopian perfectionism thoroughly infused the ideals of home and family, to produce a highly charged parent-child politics which prevails until this day. Our parental mystique is still strong.

Parents in America are supposed to be perfect, even as their

28 *Ibid.*, p. 22.
29 *Ibid.*

Father in Heaven is perfect. The divine example of the Creator is quite conscious in Christian models of parenthood. Parents are to procreate (increase and multiply), love, provide, and care for their children, just as God created man. It is a sacred duty just as one must "Honor thy father and thy mother." The early Puritans invested the father of the family with the disciplining powers of God who showed love through a proper, just chastisement. Scriptural advice on child rearing was taken literally: "Spare the rod and spoil the child." As American theological perspectives upon God's nature became more beneficent; less emphasis was given to preparing children for the Last Judgment. Love is seen as the paramount virtue and parents are to rule through love. Christ's loving sacrifice for his flock is the parents' model. A modern Pope can speak of the parental mission to provide for their offspring a paradise upon earth, to insure their thirst for the real thing. Every Christian group still stresses the primary and divinely sanctioned responsibility of parents who are charged with raising new citizens of the kingdom of God.

Secular members of American society are just as impressed with the awesome responsibility of parents to raise good citizens and good people. We all still believe that no country can be strong without good families devoted to the careful nurturing of future citizens. Bringing children up into virtue and wisdom, probity, and productivity is seen to be the most important parental task. Parents have a serious moral responsibility which is unique unto them.

There has been, however, a new and growing belief that these parental responsibilities can also be fun. The growth of a "fun morality" in the literature of child rearing has been traced.[30] Parenting will be a fun fulfillment. It is perhaps the

[30] Martha Wolfenstein, "Fun Morality: An Analysis of Recent American Child-training Literature," *The Psychoanalytic Study of the Child* (New York: International Universities Press, 1950), Vol. V, pp. 310–29.

final triumph of American optimism (and the shift from belief in a stern God who could condemn or demand sacrifice) that responsible parenthood in the Edenic home is seen as both serious and supremely pleasurable. At least this is a popular line taken by many Americans.

Only occasionally can an expert like Urie Bronfenbrenner puncture optimism with his chilling critique of American child rearing called "The Unmaking of the American Child."[31] Bronfenbrenner indicts American parents for their abdication of responsibility and consequent neglect of their children. He asserts that compared to other pro-child cultures, America is generally hostile to children's needs, despite loud cries of child worship and our supposed traditional specialization in spoiled children. This issue will be discussed later, but at this point we might say that an exclusively "fun morality" in child rearing may signal the beginning of the end of a parenting mystique.

Today there are outright challenges to majority views of parenthood on the horizon. Consider the complete rejection of the values of parenting by recent non-parenthood movements. There are also new issues connected with the biological revolution, which will take a whole chapter to discuss; but for the present it is safe to say that despite serious challenges the traditional American secular-religious consensus holds firm. Parenthood is highly valued and taken seriously as a superresponsibility. This view is so socially sanctioned that parents are given thoroughly unique legal privileges in order to carry out their task. But the qualifications for taking on the parental task are not overly scrutinized. Natural parents are good, reflecting the Creator in their procreating—that is a firm belief inside and outside religious circles. Except in the case of prospective adoptive parents, or the very poor, even a faint doctrine

---

[31] Urie Bronfenbrenner, *Two Worlds of Childhood: U.S. and U.S.S.R.* (New York: Russell Sage Foundation, 1970), pp. 95–119.

of original sin does not dim the mystique of parental goodness.

In all truth, we must say that the mystique of the good mother is more entrenched in American culture than the good father. Partly, this is because in that idyllic home in the countryside mother was protected from the contamination of the city and the evil world of competitive work. Mother also became by default the main socializer of children in the isolated home, a condition which still exists.[32] The general nineteenth-century cult of woman as the fair sex, the tender sex, the pure sex, made it inevitable that women would be the superior parent, being innately more perfect. The corollary exclusion of women from adult status and adult civil life meant that they could partake of the innocence of childhood and find an outlet for energy at home. Automatic altruism was attributed to women by virtue of their maternity and sex. Mother became a sacred word and motherhood a sacred function—with the absence of contraception or alternate careers.

The pressures upon the American woman to be a perfect parent are far greater than those on men.[33] Of course, this is also due to the past biological and social situation inherent in family survival. A great deal of maternal sacrifice was needed to carry, bear, and nurse a child to adulthood without modern medical care, nursing formulas, and penicillin. If you survived into adulthood, some woman had put incredible amounts of hard, nurturing work into your life. True, many women seem to have crumbled under the pressure: dying young, retreating into invalidism, taking to the vapours, or maybe dropping out into a disguised drug addiction (morphine for headaches, alcoholic tonics, etc.). But the more interesting and accurate con-

[32] Gerald H. Zuk, *Family Therapy: A Triadic-Based Approach* (New York: Behavioral Publications, 1971), "Wife-Mother Centrality in the American Family," pp. 117–23.
[33] Betty Friedan, *The Feminine Mystique* (New York: W. W. Norton, 1963). All of the extensive feminist literature makes the point of woman's anxiety about being a good mother.

clusion to be drawn from the evidence is the fact that many who bore the title, "my sainted mother," often deserved the name.

Fathers were also to be examples of rectitude; but while men were urged to equal the domestic virtues of women, they also were allowed their lapses into fallibility. Men could drink (openly), they could pursue independent recreation outside the home, and in the sexual sphere the double standard insured more sexual activity for men at all ages, stages, and places in the social system. A good father did not, and does not yet, have to be a paragon of perfection to the same extent as a good mother. Great sacrifices might be expected of a father in order to provide for his children and wife, but the day-to-day, constant devotional level of maternal sacrifice was not expected. Men were not required to be saints; all parents are good, but some parents are more perfect than others. Since women were generally the culture bearers, in the expressive role, and the religious inspiration of the home as well, they were more closely allied to divinity.

Although American society becomes ever more secularized, parents are not relieved of their pressures. Somehow parental responsibility is increased by a decrease in religious faith. As the culture becomes more secularized, parents are more and more on their own, part of mankind facing the universe alone without God or any divine assurance of the parents' sacred duty. A belief in evolution and natural selection of the fit certainly does not help alleviate parental responsibility. A new worry is simply added to the parental burden. Parents must be good morally and good genetically. Now they have the biological fate of the race dependent upon their reproductive behavior. Their offspring must carry good genes as well as be of sound mind, morals, and body, and happily successful.

At least the puritan religious ideology in American culture

emphasized a larger plan and purpose beyond pragmatic results. Parents must do their duty no matter what, and children
are free to make their decisions for God or accept sin as a way
of life. Parents and children have rights and duties in an ordered universe. However, with the authority of God and the
church gone from the scene, the only legitimation for a parent
is the pragmatic success of his child. The child becomes more
of a product or project, rather than an integral part of the divine plan or a unique creation of divine providence. A theology
in which worldly success rewarded goodness becomes secularized and is transferred to parent-child processes. Parents must
produce good, successful children who are healthy, wealthy,
wise, and a joy to raise. In a culture in which the Old World's
understanding of evil, fate, ambiguity, limits, and conflicts
has been partially suppressed, parental success should inevitably
follow upon will, effort, and moral goodness. In our popular
family comedies, which prevail on prime-time TV, there are
some tears, but moral goodness still prevails in the long run.

The peculiarly American forms of parenthood begin to be
seen more clearly against the background of universal problems
in the socialization of children. Americans infuse an aspiring
perfectionist work ethic into the role of parents. Children become the work of the parents and pretty much the exclusive
work of the mother's life. The dreadful specter of "Mom," or
"Mrs. Portnoy," as a neurotic monster living through and on
her children is a stock figure in popular culture. But "momism"
may be just a variant example of the dangers of what in an
institutional context Erving Goffman calls "people-work."[34]
When an institution is set up to process people (the army or
mental institutions) one finds that working on people always
threatens to become too much like working on objects and
things. Efficiency, success, and the product become primary—

[34] Erving Goffman, *Asylums* (Garden City, N.Y.: Doubleday & Co.,
1961), p. 74.

especially when it is the family and its child in question; a child after all is "unshaped," "unformed," and quite powerless.

So in America parents inevitably worry about how their children "will turn out." Will the end product do? Will the right techniques work? Since the intensity and self-scrutiny of parent-child processes are at a high level, due to isolation, mobility, and more available information, a great deal of anxiety is generated. All parents everywhere probably partake of certain amounts and kinds of parental anxiety in their roles of providing, surviving, and socializing. Harry Stack Sullivan speaks of the inevitable anxiety of a mother about being a good mother to her child in the eyes of her social group.[35] But surely Americans, beset by perfectionism, rapid change, mobility and productivity goals, including "fun," may be among the most anxious of all parents. Although there are inevitable inherent limits and conflicts built into the parenting process, no quarter is given to parents by themselves or others. As Robert Coles observes: "Parents [today] are often enough resented and never forgiven for all their failures of omission or commission."[36] The good things don't count; winning is everything.

Perhaps in the end the most characteristic and enduring problem of American parents seeking perfection in themselves and their children is the constant change and mobility of our society. How does one raise children to succeed in an unknown future in an unknown place? Margaret Meade has suggested that the young must now teach the old in new ways, but Erik Erikson describes the more classic American dilemma:

The same families, the same mothers, were forced to prepare men and women who would take root in the community life

[35] Harry Stack Sullivan, *The Collected Works of Harry Stack Sullivan* (New York: W. W. Norton, 1953), Vol. I, p. 53.
[36] Robert Coles, "Shrinking History—Part One," *The New York Review of Books*, 20 (February 22, 1973), p. 20.

and the gradual class stratification of the new villages and towns and at the same time to prepare these children for the possible physical hardships of homesteading on the frontiers. . . . They must be prepared for any number of extreme opposites in milieu, and always ready to seek new goals and to fight for them in merciless competition.[37]

In this process mothers must not weaken potential frontiersmen by "protective maternalism." Independence, initiative, toughness, adaptability, and drive were necessary for survival. But at the same time an ideal of parental goodness and the standards of paradise are increasingly introduced through the cult of home and family. How do you create a paradise from which a tough competitive frontiersman or future man emerges? Home has still got to be some place you leave in order to make it. Perfect parents must produce a paradise from which perfect children will happily press to who knows what. Ties with the past and past models can't be trusted, so even the model of the perfect home must be constantly reinvented by parents. Widespread affluence and parental freedom from drudgery simply increase the problems by increasing the available alternatives, options, and decisions.

How much easier the parental responsibilities of affluent classes in the past can look! In Jane Austen's novels, eighteenth-century standards of responsible parenthood mainly decreed that affluent parents provide "livings" for their children. All you had to do was hand children an independent income, property, and a house so that they could marry and raise a family without any unseemly grubbing about in trade or professions. Alas, such dependence, with its repudiation of work in a meritocracy is shocking to American ideals of independence, work, and achievement. In America not even the upper upper classes

[37] Erik H. Erikson, *Childhood and Society*, 2d. ed. (New York: W. W. Norton, 1963), p. 293.

can buy their way out of parenting, no matter how much money and property they can dispense to their children. No American success story begins with wealth unless it ends with achievements à la Rockefeller, Roosevelt, or Kennedy.

Other parents in other cultures may never have felt so much pressure to be good parents, with so little certainty or control. The whole history of America, our whole culture, has made certain that anxiety over success and aspirations toward perfection prevail. American parents are still very much affected by their peculiar history. Utopian aspirations to perfect parenthood are stronger than ever, along with the underside of such a demand for perfection, the drop-out phenomena. If you can't win, give up. Another change, which is rapidly taking place, produces fathers who are as involved in parenthood as mothers, just as the nineteenth-century cult prescribed. With the addition of more and more men to the ranks, more parents than ever before are seeking an answer to the question: How can I be a good parent? With foolhardy daring and American optimism intact (good is not perfect), I shall try to describe what good parents do in the following chapter.

What Does a Good Parent Do?

Many parents today are not terribly interested in histories of parenthood, nor in the cultural context of parenthood with its politics and controversies; but they are concerned about *being* good parents. When they ask questions about parenting, they are usually referring to themselves and the central question: "What does a good parent do?"

Parents like the rest of mankind seek not only intellectual truth, but aspire as well to be good. Few people succeed in suppressing completely some search for value; we want to be wise, upright, righteous. Almost every culture has an informing image of the good man, the good woman, the good life. And as we see in our American tradition, perfectionist images of the saintly mother and the good father have been very deeply imbedded in our values.

But there has been very little fusion of role-images into "the good parent," or "good parents." Male roles and female roles have been so polarized in the past that parenting per se was not imagined. The good mother was thought to be quite different from the good father and had quite a different parental function for the child. The ideal of equal, co-operating, unified

However, no observer of life in America could not but note growing problems in basic parental protectiveness. Good nutrition, medical care, and the physical safety of children cannot be assumed any more. A shocking amount of parental neglect and lack of protection is creeping into our culture and lifestyles. Much of this neglect remains hidden and ironically glossed over by talk of "momism" and "maternal overprotection." As a leading observer of American family life very acutely observes:

All cultures and all families institutionalize norms of protectiveness, and the tendency of our culture to lose them is expressed in the fact that while psychiatry is preoccupied with overprotection, it has shown relatively little interest in underprotection.[1]

Parental protection of a child (or anyone else) involves an ability to "perceive the interconnections between time, space, motion, light and darkness, objects and people" as well as an ability to "perceive the actual dangers and make the effort to protect somebody."[2] A parent may not be able to protect for many personal reasons (because he is afraid, because he dissociates his fear, because he wants to hurt himself, and so on). But within our culture, underprotection and the loss of protective norms often stem from overconfidence, overdependency on specialists and technology, and a decline in an ability to cope with the social environment which becomes ever more complex as it falls apart. A prime instance of the problem can be seen in the difficulty of procuring medical care and protection.

Much medical care is inadequate because so few physicians

[1] Jules Henry, *Pathways to Madness* (New York: Random House, 1971), p. 23.
[2] *Ibid.*

are available for general family practice. Preventive medicine is all important in insuring children's health and it is much better when the doctor knows the family and can communicate with the parents and children. Clearly, continuous observation and continuity aid in patient care, before and during a medical crisis.

Yet medical specialization and patient mobility destroy continuity, while the pressure of numbers takes away the individualized attention necessary. Many medical problems which could be prevented may simply be overlooked because of infrequent, hurried, and inadequate examinations, and there is always pressure toward speedy, efficient cures with miracle drugs. Parents may be paying high fees to a variety of medical specialists and getting indifferent care.

Many physicians are educated into a heroic, crisis-centered image of themselves and are bored with their practice. Medical emergencies are more interesting to them, for health is not so challenging as disease. Concentrating upon the crises takes less patience than the careful observation needed for the earliest detection of problems. Many a parent has been falsely reassured or had their own observations and opinions dismissed, to the detriment of their child's health. People have been taught to be acquiescent to the doctor's orders (and to other professional experts).

Physicians can encourage an overdependency upon their authority. They are the powerful knowledgeable ones who will heal with their magic medical arsenal while parents and other laymen know little. Since most physicians are males and most parental contacts are made with mothers, there can be further distortions of communication. Instead of encouraging maternal independence, judgment and activity, doctors often expect traditional feminine submissiveness on top of patient acquiescence.

Parents, who after all *are* laymen, are in a most vulnerable position vis-à-vis the professional medical establishment (as well as with other professionals). To ensure the proper protection of their children, they have to avoid neglect on the one hand and an overdependency upon the professional physician and the technology of miracle drugs on the other. When unsatisfactory physician-patient relationships create a negative reaction there's a strong tendency (as in the youthful counterculture, or among the poor) to withdraw totally from medical care. In communes settled on the land, babies are born without nurse or doctor and the followers of folk medicine everywhere increase. Perhaps the movements among physicians to restore family practice and take a more whole-patient approach may solve problems in procuring health. A rejection of traditional Western medicine and the doctor has its own dangers.

Parental overconfidence in nature and the natural way can also be dangerous for children. Reactions against cleanliness and the previous generations' fight against germs can result in new dangers (hepatitis, venereal disease, and body lice among the young for instance). Parental carelessness about vaccinations, shots, contagion, and personal hygiene may be justified "ideologically," but it is still inexcusable carelessness. Home nursing is a lost skill although careful nursing when a child is ill is still important to good health since nature cannot always cure without help. Overconfident dependence upon drugs, doctors, hospitals, or nature does not encourage proper parental protection of a child's health.

If medical care of children is not in a good state, the American child's need for nutrition, sleep, and exercise is in much greater disarray. While more people may know more about nutrition than ever before, more children are eating miserably. Those who are not nutritionally illiterate have to remember that memorizing charts of the seven basic foods one needs for a well-balanced diet is not the same as eating these foods. Nor, in most homes, is the question one of affording good food. In fact, it is often the opposite problem. With affluence and the changing character of food, many children have access to a constant supply of candy, sweets, soda pop, and ice cream as well as a multitude of snack foods. As Dr. Jean Mayer, the noted authority on nutrition, says, "Malnourishment, whether caused by poverty or improper diet, contributes to the alarming health situation in the United States today."[3] Mayer is particularly worried about young people who eat more of the new snack foods which have not been enriched enough to be nourishing. As usual, nutrition and lifestyle are connected.

The ban upon eating between meals, or even immediately before dinner, has become a thing of the past in many families. Unfortunately even the family meal has often become a thing of the past. Fewer and fewer families sit down together for a meal in which they all start together to eat one menu at the same time. Children, adults, and adolescents more and more eat separately or simply snack on the run. More children eat from the icebox irregularly than you might expect. Are their parents all depending upon vitamins?

These changing eating habits have come to the notice of those studying the habits of Americans. Studies have been done on the number of minutes American families spend together at family meals (fewer and fewer). As noted an authority as Margaret Meade has even recommended that as a culture we should change over to the pattern of eating small amounts when hungry instead of the traditional three meals a day.

Of course there is nothing sacred about three meals a day, and it may be much more healthy actually to eat less more frequently during a day. However, in other cultures in which people nourish themselves with frequent small portions there is not a plethora of junk food. When American children eat constantly they are eating mostly unnutritious foods which become

[3] Jean Mayer, "Toward a National Nutrition Policy," *Science*, Vol. 176, No. 4032 (April 21, 1972), p. 239.

substitutes for needed food. They learn to prefer the less nutritious from high-powered commercials on TV and from the practice of their peers. Excessive tooth decay in children is one obvious result of the abdication of parental supervision of diet. We seem to have gone directly from a culture in which children were forced to clean their plates and eat their spinach to complete abdication of parental control and concern.

Older studies of the middle-class child's eating situation are rapidly becoming dated. There used to be depicted an anxiety-ridden child whose parents were forcing him to eat, eat, eat, while at the same time strictly enforcing table manners and "correct" behavior at the table. Parental power and eating were so fused that resistance to food and parents became the same. The predictable "eating problems" which resulted from parental power displays were often contrasted with the healthy chaos of kibbutz children eating without their parents and with their peers.

Maybe the picture of anxious parental harassment at table is still valid for many Americans, but we seem more rapidly approaching a fragmented eating style. Unlike the kibbutz children who were still supervised by adults in a highly organized routine and nutritional scheme, many American children, especially adolescents, have dispensed with all family meals. They eat what they want, when they want it. If man in his natural state ever had an instinct for eating a balanced diet, surely that was before he was weaned on candy, chips, and soda pop.

Here again there has been a violent cultural reaction in the rise of the health-food movement. Nutrition becomes a major concern among advocates of natural foods. Healthy cooking and eating becomes a preoccupation, with new eating rituals substituted for older middle-class manners and traditions. Parents and other consumers can learn a lot from this movement. Nutrition and diet are important to health and well-being.

Nourishment and the establishment of good eating habits are a prime parental concern. Feeding the young well from fetus to adolescent is a major function of parents. The necessity of good nutrition is the basis for other developments. For parents to abdicate dietary supervision in an overreaction to past scarcity and strictness is a form of underprotection.

Parental care in ensuring proper sleep and exercise is also waning. There are kindergartens where the children are tired because they have been watching TV until nine or ten o'clock at night. Elementary schools in rich suburbs regularly send home pleas to the parents to see that their children get more rest. Granted that it is ridiculous for an urbanized culture to be operating on work and school schedules inherited from the early rising of the farm, yet since we do, we must get our children to bed early enough to avoid their constant fatigue.

Children who do not get enough sleep are unable to learn, they are often accident prone, and generally more susceptible to illness. A parent who wishes to protect his child properly must enforce a routine that includes enough sleep. Parents have to fight the good fight against excessive TV-watching in the interest of sleep and also in the cause of enough exercise. Rested children are less likely to languish in front of the TV in the afternoon after school.

There are actually suburban neighborhoods in which the children do not ever come out to play. They are eating in front of the TV and cannot be budged. Many children hardly walk anywhere. Lessons in every sport and gym classes in school cannot make up for the lack of sustained daily exercise. The shocking results of American children upon fitness tests (which started a national campaign for fitness) stem directly from a lack of parental push in exercise. In the area of physical fitness permissive parental overprotection can be no protection. Parents have to protect their child's health by forbidding so much physical passivity. Children who are not naturally prone to exercise and outdoor play have to be encouraged. The best protection for adult health is for a child to learn to be active with his parents as they go about an active life. Children who no longer can work with their parents on the farm or have necessary chores to do can find substitute ways to exercise. The leisure explosion of camping, hiking, bicycling, and other outdoor sports should not be scorned. If necessity doesn't force us to become physically fit, then we have to self-consciously initiate regular physical activity.

Parental encouragement of physical competence has always been part of ensuring our children's safety. Quick reflexes, ability to swim, competence in bicycling, running, sports, and endurance—all such things protect a child's safety. But there is one complicating factor in the development of physical competence in our culture. Early in life a toddler should have the freedom to explore, investigate, and practice physical skills, yet the environment in which we live is so complex, that it is highly dangerous to let a child have the freedom he needs. The ordinary home is a booby trap for the toddler and small child. Electrical outlets, the bathtub, the stove, appliances, cleaning agents, medicines, and of course the omnipresent automobile, present countless dangers. Protecting an active climbing, crawling, curious child is a full-time job. The terrible statistics showing that more children die in home accidents than from disease points to the difficulty of the task.[4] Physical safety for children has to be a constant concern and is rarely taken seriously enough. Neither, ironically, is the small child's need for active exploration given enough importance.

It's the worst of all worlds for a small child. We encourage passive confinement in various contraptions, infant seats, feeding tables, car seats, high chairs, playpens, cribs, for long periods of time, and then do not give enough thought to safety in the

[4] E. A. Suchman and A. L. Scherzer, *Current Research in Childhood Accidents* (New York: Association for the Aid of Crippled Children, 1960).

rest of the environment. We imprison the baby instead of babyproofing the house. Preparing the environment and giving constant supervision to active children is best. Yet mothers are encouraged to keep their houses, possessions, and clothes clean and bright instead of supervising and encouraging the play of their children. Other children are turned out of doors, despite the dangers of automobiles, while the all-important housework is being done. Parental priorities are skewed; we need to recognize that high housekeeping standards and child rearing are incompatible, and inevitably conflict. The same children who are locked out of spotless houses are also encouraged to sit and watch TV indoors in order to keep the house clean.

Too few parents in this country have gotten the message that they need to initiate activity *and* supervise for safety. Actually, accidents and unstimulated apathy go together. Bored children who are not being encouraged in exercise or creative activity that channels energy can be driven to dangerous activities. Underprotection can begin with passive parents understimulating children. Occasionally daring parents, obsessed with independence and risk-taking, underprotect children (mostly sons) by pushing them too hard. These are also parents who underprotect in the name of misguided permissiveness. They trust too much in the child's capacities or they cannot take the trouble or bear to frustrate and control the child. The negative imperatives of good parental protection involve having and inculcating fear of real dangers, having the ability to inflict necessary pain (as in vaccination and shots), and being able to frustrate and control dangerous activity. Out of sight, out of mind is no principle for parents. All of the advanced technology, which makes our lives so much easier in many many ways, makes safeguarding our children more difficult.

This changing parental situation could be a world-wide phenomenon. Once a visitor from Italy was reminiscing about his own rural childhood. His mother had taken him as a baby and later as a child into the fields with her as she helped her husband on the farm. Caring for her many children in this way did not present as many problems as caring for her one new grandson who lived in the same village, now complete with cars and modern technology. Could it be that technology has not freed parents as much as we would like to think? At least it is a double-edged sword in many respects. Have the marvelous advances in medicine which have lowered the infant-mortality rate been partly offset by the dangers in the house and on the streets? Unanswerable question.

*The main point to be made is that the good parent's protection and nurturing of children is no easy task. Basic, elementary physical protection and the provision of necessities is not solved by affluence. Nor do the plethora of specialists in our society relieve parents of their protecting function. Protecting a child and caring for him physically still takes an enormous amount of energy and more and more intelligence. Parental aggression and dominance is needed in order to cope. To procure from an increasingly complex environment what the child needs, and to protect the child in the environment, takes action, initiative, and aggression. Active nurturing is called for in response to the new organism's helplessness. Aggressive parental protection buys time and safety for the child's development. Parenting is "a buffering process."[5]

Furthermore, in providing "necessities" in an ordered competent way, the parent from the beginning organizes a child's views of his environment. Time, space, and objects will be perceived as orderly or chaotic depending on the parent's ability to organize and actively cope with the material environment.

[5] Jerome S. Bruner, "The Uses of Immaturity," *Social Change and Human Behavior*, ed. by George V. Coelho and Eli A. Rubinstein (Maryland: National Institute of Mental Health, 1972), p. 7.

The parental ordering of material life affects a child's perception of the world. Understanding cause-and-effect relationships, how you "make things happen," comes from a child's observation of his parents' activity. Parental choices in housing, clothing, furnishings, decorations, etc., and how they are arranged and used, influence a child's future perceptions and expectancies; parents create a world in microcosm. But what else besides proper physical protection and the creation of order is essential in good parenting? •

Plenty, of course. The parent-child relationship is so intimate that every caretaking function is charged with an emotional dimension. Human beings are so complicated that there are many things going on at once in any interaction. We operate with many channels "on" at once. What is being done, or being said, is only a part of the message. Tone of voice, gestures, facial expressions, muscle tone, posture, timing, spacing, and rhythm are all ways that we communicate with one another. (And maybe smell?)[6] As we all know, from experience, "It's not so much what he said, or did, but the *way* it was done that made the difference." All the more so in parent-child interchanges.

In human relationships there is an atmosphere which has nothing to do with the weather outside. We speak of these feelings in the imagery of temperature and climate. "What a chilly reception that was!" Or one might feel very relaxed and welcome in a "warm" family. There are also "stormy" relationships and ones in which undercurrents are active. Intuitively we understand this but when we try to analyze "warmth" and "coldness" in feelings and impressions we have more difficulty.

"Cold" connotes distance, rigidity, displeasure, lack of attention, and personal involvement. A cold or cool family would be one in which if there was not active hostility, at least no one

[6] Mark L. Knapp, *Nonverbal Communication in Human Interaction* (New York: Holt, Rinehart & Winston, 1972).

much noticed or cared about the others beyond the minimum demands, perhaps, of duty. An absent, empty atmosphere is colder than cold.

"Warmth" on the other hand, connotes a human closeness, pliancy, pleasure, attention, attachment, tenderness, and deep common involvement. A "warm" parent-child relationship connotes involvement and mutual pleasure. The parent and child, or parents and children, are close, give lots of attention to each other and take pleasure in presence. There is playfulness as well as seriousness on the scene. The whole atmosphere is relaxed and without strain and tension. As those in the counterculture would say, the vibrations are good.

The infant and small child is particularly sensitive to the emotional atmosphere of the people around him. Before language can be understood, there is preverbal communication throughout feeding and handling routines.[7] Parental attitudes and feelings, especially about the body and its functions, are communicated in many ways very early. Harry Stack Sullivan even speaks of a process of emotional "contagion" between infant and mother or caretaker.[8] The infant "catches" the attitudes and feelings of the caretaker; he senses the prevailing emotions. I think there is obviously a lot of truth in this idea of emotional contagion, or atmosphere, although it can hardly be fully explained. Non-verbal communication does seem to operate as a major factor in parent-child relationships. From the nursing infant to the adolescent, subtle communications of attitudes and expectations make a difference. Deep parental despair and rejection as well as hope and acceptance can be conveyed to a child. Other basic attitudes are also transmitted.

[7] Ray L. Birdwhistell, *Kinesics and Context Essays on Body Motion Communication* (Philadelphia: University of Pennsylvania Press, 1970), Part I, "Learning to Be a Human Body," pp. 3–64.
[8] Harry Stack Sullivan, *Conceptions of Modern Psychiatry* (New York: W. W. Norton, 1953), p. 17.

Theories which say that the child acts out the parents' deep unstated wishes and problems are built on the premise that parental wishes can somehow be transmitted and communicated. Filming or videotaping family interactions in therapy reveal subtle non-verbal reinforcements and encouragements, silencing strategies and refusals between family members.[9]

The thought that our personal parental problems or hidden messages are being communicated to our children is deeply disturbing. However, if communication *is* going on at deep non-verbal levels, we do well to remember that the good as well as the bad will be communicated. Deep aspirations to be good and loving and deep caring may be communicated as well as anxieties, aggressions, and rejections. Who's to say latent goodness may not be by far the most influential? The good parent is one who cares, who tries to care ever more deeply and wisely, and doesn't dwell too much on whatever may be going on without awareness. We can try to be more conscious of what we do, but unless things go very badly, there's enough to be done in parenting with a will. Consciously trying to be really available to a child has a built-in momentum.

A parent willing to take the time to give sustained attention to his child opens the way to spontaneous warmth and enjoyment. Watching a child carefully lets a parent sense not only what is needed for protection, but what a loving human partner for the child should do at a particular moment. Partnership is the essence of good parenthood, an accommodation to the changing needs of the child. One of the most important parental partnering functions involves language development.[10] A dialogue between child and caretaker is essential. As the child hears the adult answer and elaborate speech, he is able

[9] Gerald H. Zuk, *Family Therapy: A Triadic-Based Approach* (New York: Behavioral Publications, 1971).

[10] Roger Brown, *Social Psychology* (New York: The Macmillan Co., 1965), "Language: The System and Its Acquisition," pp. 246–349.

to master his native language and a host of other related skills.[11] Parental response makes a responsive child.

From playing peek-a-boo to supporting career plans, the good parent entices and encourages the child into social life. As the first human partners in playing all games, learning all skills, and meeting all problems, good parents initiate and sustain an ongoing dialogue. There may be many different styles of parent-child dialogues which succeed.[12] Since satisfactory human dialogue is a joy, a good parent introduces his child to the goodness of life. Life seems worth while despite inevitable struggles and set backs. Providing social pleasure and enjoyment are an all-important part of parenting. Almost no one takes parental obligations to give joy and pleasure seriously enough. A child needs pleasure, games, joy, and play.

A little girl in her open way delivers a precious accolade when she says to her mother: "I love you and Daddy. I'm glad I was born." An essential goal of human parenthood is just that: to make our children glad they were born and eager for life. All of the protective care and nurture in good parenting should reinforce the mutual warmth, acceptance, and valuing we call love. Physical protection, partnering and care will be a dimension of the commitment that gives loving security and vice versa. A child needs security and a background confidence to his life.

Good parents try to make despair impossible; they give the basic trust and hope necessary, at the beginning of life. At any age you give another trust and hope by reaching him with the believable news that there's a world with people in it worth living for. The future will not be self-enclosed or limited to the present situation; change comes. A parent conveys hope and

[11] Jean Piaget, *The Language and Thought of the Child* (New York: Humanities Press, 1959).

[12] Selma Fraiberg, "The Origins of Human Bonds," *Commentary* (December 1967), p. 55.

basic trust to his child in the same way, only without much of a concept of "future" to work with. It may be that the infant at the beginning does not have any sense of self, either. He may be very much untogether, not even recognizing his body as his own, much less other people as other.[13]

Our study of infancy has just begun and a fascinating work it is. Do infants see objects and how early? When do they begin to think, or have emotions? How does the self come to consciousness? Psychologists are struggling to find out. Penetrating the infancy barrier takes real ingenuity, as well as sophisticated research techniques. But parents are not psychologists, and parenting and studying an infant are not the same thing. Parents participate directly, they must respond directly. The quality and quantity of parental response, the parents' part in the infant-parent dialogue is crucial in establishing basic trust and hope.

The parent communicates directly through presence and caretaking. When the infant cries the parent acts. When the infant is hungry he is fed, when cold, he's warmed, when wet he's dried, dirt is cleaned, bubbles burped, restlessness is rocked, and so on. In addition to caretaking through touch and feeding, there is the parental presence of face, voice, and control of the environment. The point of parental care and presence is to give what is appropriate to the need of the infant, *in response to* the infant's activity.[14]

In all probability the infant's sense of self is created or at least strengthened when his acts produce response. He gradually develops an expectancy of order, a hope, a sense of the future. An infant's repeated experiences of his act begetting a response may establish a consciousness of his self in the

[13] Gordon W. Allport, *Becoming: Basic Considerations for a Psychology of Personality* (New Haven: Yale University Press, 1955), 11, "The Propium," pp. 41–56.

[14] Bruno Bettelheim, *The Empty Fortress: Infantile Autism and the Birth of the Self* (New York: Macmillan, 1968), "A Reason To Act," pp. 51–57.

world.[15] Who can say whether this first consciousness of self is oceanic bliss, or a sense of omnipotence? At least it is the beginning of an "I" who is aware of existence in space and time, a world of cause and effect peopled with others. An "I" or ego is confirmed by being answered or addressed by another. The continuing dialogue confirms the self by being an experience of self-existence.

Experience with things in the environment is also important. Interaction with external objects may help the emerging self to know that one's body is separate from the surroundings and can act autonomously, at will. The painstaking observations of Piaget, the Swiss genius of child psychology, have shown that infants from the beginning of life are experimenting and learning from experience.[16] The growth of intelligence progresses as inner capacities and experience grow; and much of this important childhood experience arises because parents have intervened or prepared the environment. Parents provide cribs, blankets, toys, lights, sounds, and many of the other stimuli in an infant's world.

Another vital parental role is to create barriers against overwhelming stimuli. Overloading a child's capacities to handle and process information and experience is as damaging as understimulating him. Parents as protective buffers do have to censor and select stimuli as best they can. Interacting with things and people, building up experience over a period of time, is crucial in creating a self-image. Parents must see that the experience is appropriate for the unique child in a unique situation.

When Dr. Sylvia Brody studied patterns of mothering by watching mothers care for their babies, she judged the quality of the caretaking on three criteria. These were frequency of

[15] *Ibid.*
[16] Jean Piaget, *The Origins of Intelligence in Children* (New York: International Universities Press, 1952).

care, the sensitivity of care, and the consistency of the care.[17] All were necessary for good mothering, or indeed, as I would say, good parenting at all ages, since a father could also respond in the same ways to his child. Frequency, sensitivity, and consistency are necessary, for without frequent enough care the child will not get enough of what is needed. If the care is inconsistent and unpatterned, no expected patterns of trust or comprehension can be built up by the child toward the environment. If the care is not sensitive to the real need of the particular child, then it is as frustrating as no response at all.

A combined balance of frequency, consistency, and sensitivity is needed in good parental response. Frequent consistent care, for instance, that is insensitive may let the parent feel that he or she is doing what they think should be done, but is a total failure from the child's point of view, if it is not sensitive to the child's real need. If, on the other hand, the care is too sensitive and frequent without any consistency, emotional confusion can be the result. Parenting skill is based upon a mature parental personality able to bear the stress of caring for the demands of a child along with general knowledge of child care.

Intellectual understanding of the parent-child situation is a help, but not nearly so important as the personal ability to have empathy and intuit what a child needs at the moment. Deciding what parental action should be taken depends first on the ability to sense what the baby or child needs or wants from his point of view. In other words one must be able to imaginatively project one's self into another's skin, to be one's child, and imagine a separate personhood and point of view. If a parent is too rigid, unimaginative, egoistic, or anxious, this

---

[17] Sylvia Brody, *Patterns of Mothering: Maternal Influence During Infancy* (New York: International Universities Press, 1956); Harry Stack Sullivan listed the three essentials as "consistency," "frequency," and "sanity."

seems an impossible task, but usually for most normal, healthy persons, it comes fairly naturally. Perhaps some latent remembrance of childhood or identification with one's own parents[18] informs the imagination; or there is some innate human ability to identify with others as really *other*, and understand *their* non-verbal cues of pain, pleasure, need, and so on. Infants may bring to the fore special human capacities for discrimination and tender empathetic responses.[19]

However, the ability to imaginatively be one's child is not enough in parenting. The parent must also at the same time be the adult parent who knows more than the child about reality. Knowing the world and being aware of the future and necessity, the parent must also restrict, restrain, and enforce unpleasantness when the good of the child is at stake. The negative side of protection appears again. The parents who empathized with the pain of a child so much that they neglected inoculations or controls would have carried empathy too far. An adult who is still a child emotionally cannot carry out the responsibilities of parenthood, especially the painful unpleasant duties, or those requiring adult competence in society.

A good parent is one who from his child's infancy to adulthood can be fairly adept at the double emotional life. He can understand his child through empathy and yet remain the adult who must do what is best for the child. A parent cannot lose himself in the child or become a child himself. Part of what is best in the long run is inevitably going to involve frustration of child and parent. Giving protection or even pleasure may not be pleasant for the parent. Parental control and limiting is absolutely necessary to the child's growing process. A child

[18] Rose W. Coleman, Ernst Kris, and Sally Provence, "The Study of Variations of Early Parental Attitudes," *The Psychoanalytic Study of the Child* (New York: International Universities Press, 1953), Vol. VIII.

[19] Michael Argyle, *Social Interaction* (Chicago and New York: Aldine Atherton, 1969), p. 49.

who is never frustrated or inhibited would be impossible to
live with and ill-prepared to survive in the world. Just as having
some fear and distrust protect a child, so an ability to handle
frustration and conflict is absolutely necessary for coping with
reality.[20]

Still, a major parental concern is not to frustrate a growing
child too much, or in ways which are particularly damaging to
him. A great deal of wise discrimination is necessary, for every
child is unique and needs stimulation, protection, and discipline suited to him. There are undoubtedly quite different
types of temperament in children just as there are differences
in every other inherited characteristic. The old behaviorist
dogma which asserted that any baby could be made into anything by environmental conditioning has been discredited. It's
rather a process of inheritance interacting with environmental
experience which shapes a personality. And each building-up
of experience shapes the further experience available to the
unique child.[21]

A child may be highly active, or very calm and easy-going, or
of mixed temperament. His rhythmicity, perceptions, body
functioning, ability to make transitions and reactions to stimuli
and frustration may be quite unique.[22] A highly excitable baby,
for instance, may need a calm atmosphere and less stimulation
in order to have his attention engaged and focused, while a
slowly aroused baby may need much more social interaction in
order to become engaged in his environment. As in caretaking
routines, the parent's partnering should be adjusted to the
baby and child's unique needs. When babies have been studied
from birth to school age, different patterns of individual differ-

[20] Bettelheim, *op. cit.*
[21] Sybille K. Escalona, "Patterns of Infantile Experience and the Developmental Process," *The Psychoanalytic Study of the Child,* Vol. XVIII
(New York: International Universities Press, 1963), pp. 197–265.
[22] *Ibid.*

ences become apparent.[23] There may even be children with "difficult" temperaments who are very hard to partner because of the unevenness of their response, high sensitivity to stimuli, negative responses to novelty, and low tolerances for frustration. ("Easy" babies have the opposite temperamental characteristics.)[24]

Whatever the temperament, when caretaking and parental efforts do not succeed in meeting a child's needs, parents may lose confidence, lose patience and compound the problem by expecting the worst. Parental frustration and a sense of failure can arise more easily if parents think they are responsible for every reaction of the child. A more realistic appraisal of the child's innate uniqueness and a better understanding of how parent and child interact help. A specific parental personality and temperament may also be hard to adjust to the specific temperament of the child. In something as neutral as activity level, for instance, a slow parent and a highly active, quick child may have difficulty adjusting to each other. Some parents also will be better adjusting to certain stages than others. Individual parental personalities make it easier for some to parent babies, others to handle school-age children. (Toddlers and adolescents seem easy only to superparents, I'm sure.) But the parent is an adult; it is the parent who must adapt and be more objective about his own subjective responses. Parents have to be grown up and run the family since children can't. The good parent persists in love, affection, and caretaking even when emotional rewards are not immediately forthcoming. Perseverance is a parental necessity; each day is a fresh start approached with hope, not hopeless helplessness and old resentments.

Parents need to be committed to the uneven, one-way giv-

[23] Alexander Thomas, Stella Chess, and Herbert G. Birch, "The Origin of Personality," *Scientific American*, Vol. 223 (August 1970), pp. 102–9.
[24] *Ibid.*

ing which parenthood often entails. Self-confidence and consistent commitment as a parent cannot depend on positive feelings or instant gratification. Part of the parental role is to be constantly challenged. Today, parent-child conflict is inevitable and essential, for the development of an independent personal autonomy on the part of the child is all-important. He must be able to test his will against his parents and come to feel his own strength. Through trust in his parents, he can learn to trust himself. If there is not a close bond of love and trust, a deep sense of security, the child will be too cowed, too anxious, to develop his own autonomy or express anger. A child can be too submissive, too good, too much an extension of his parents' will and ego, never separating from his parents to become an individual.[25] Learning to handle conflict and hostility is an important lesson. To recognize anger and see adversaries as they really are here and now are marks of maturity. A parent who copes with his own anger well can help a child do the same and not be threatened. Home is also where you learn to fight well and be angry when it's appropriate.

A beloved parent who is doing a good job will be challenged, and there will be conflict. A young personality emerges and takes shape in a constant testing and a constant pressure against parental will and authority. Individual will and personal initiative may first develop in the second year of life with a toddler's new mobility,[26] but the struggle for independence and an emerging separate identity goes on until the child comes to adulthood. The terrible twos may be relived in adolescent-parent conflicts. A good parent is able to be strong, confident, and exert authority, in order to come to mutual solutions of

[25] Margaret S. Mahler, Fred Pine, and Anni Bergman, "The Mother's Reaction to Her Toddler's Drive for Individuation," *Parenthood: Its Psychology and Psychopathology*, ed. by E. James Anthony and Therese Benedek (Boston: Little, Brown & Co., 1970), pp. 257–74.
[26] *Ibid.*

problems,[27] without crushing his child or driving him to self-destruction. In a delicate balancing act, good leadership both exerts power and encourages resistance and independence. Mutual pride and mutual respect between parent and child build strong egos even capable of making mistakes without undue guilt. Parents have to let children make their own mistakes and have their own guilt.

The great test of any good leader and parent is how well you develop another's ability to act and lead. Partly this comes from expecting enough of the right things at the right times from a child and not underrating his intelligence. Nor can a child's intelligence be misled and confused. It is important in a family that parents call things for what they are, recognize social sham as sham,[28] and not communicate in confusing contradictory ways. Perceiving the world clearly and not denying reality is an all-important parental capacity that is passed on to children. Honesty and truth telling in a family have as much adaptive value as love and care. Parental confusion and self-deceit are also catching. Good parents try hard not to make contradictory demands (double binds),[29] give different messages on different channels (smiling reproofs), or tell lies. Honesty helps keep parents and children in touch with their own experience, and cuts down on family secrets which have to be suppressed.

Truth telling, however, does not mean applying absolute critical standards to a child's efforts. In a good parent there's a high capacity for appreciation of his child. Besides being a partner the parent is a child's first audience—his first listener, his first viewer, his first reader reactor. Harry Stack Sullivan felt that everyone carried around in his psyche an imaginary

27 Dr. Thomas Gordon, *Parent Effectiveness Training* (New York: Peter H. Wyden, 1970), 11, "The 'No-Lose' Method for Resolving Conflicts," pp. 194–215.
28 Jules Henry, *Pathways to Madness, op. cit.,* pp. 181–82.
29 *Ibid.,* p. 192.

observer as perpetual viewer, listener, and reader of his own actions, words, and writing.[30] If one feels that the observer is highly critical and rejecting, then it is difficult to talk, or act, or write. A child who has an expectancy that he will be heard, seen, and read with pleasure has a lifetime of functioning made easier. A good parent gives a child both at home and at endless recitals, school plays, graduations, and athletic events, a welcoming audience for all his efforts. Parental applause and appreciation lingers on for life, as does parental indifference and disapproval.

A good parent delights in this unique child. He appreciates everything about him. He attributes value to his child and naturally builds a positive self-image. Even the things that create trouble and more work, such as high energy or great creative endeavors involving water, paint, clay, and later other materials and noisy projects, are welcome signs of the child's health and good spirits. The child's struggles for independence and autonomy are also good signs. In America, every child must be able to leave home and make it on his own through work and initiative. Facing life when parents are no longer there to help is the crucial test of how well the parent raised his child. The home environment cannot so overprotect the child that he cannot function in any way but as the child of his parents.

The first test of how well a child has been prepared comes from his relationships with his peers. Good parents understand the child's need for peers for their child, and from an early age try to provide playmates and friends. As families become smaller and the old extended family gives way to the mobile nuclear family, the problem of finding enough playmates becomes more difficult but more imperative. No parent can give to a child the experiences available from his age-mates or older

[30] Sullivan, *The Interpersonal Theory of Psychiatry* (New York: W. W. Norton, 1953), p. 239.

children. Much of the new research in child development has stressed the heretofore-neglected influence of a child's friends and peer group.[31]

Children learn from other children. Other children can communicate with a child as no parent or adult ever can. Open classrooms and revolutionary new reading programs make use of children teaching their fellows. Also, it appears that other children can even assuage the loss of parents if mutual ties between children are strong and continuous. Not only can parentless baby monkeys play each other to health, but parentless children from World War II's concentration camps were able to help each other when they were kept together as a group.[32] The mutual affection and bonds of kibbutz children raised together is another instance of the vital and positive influence of children upon one another.

We can see that in our culture, children living with their parents will have their peers more or less chosen by their parents' social situation. Housing, schools, urban or suburban or rural lifestyles present different situations for a child. The economic situation and the status of the parents make a huge difference in the child's group. However, even the most successful parent can do no more than provide the opportunity for good peer relationships. As in so many things the parent can set-up a situation, but the child must take the initiative himself. Parents cannot make friends for their children. It's again one of the situations in which parents can create a favorable context, but not make something happen. Parental activity often has to be followed by strategic passivity.

A child must get along with his peers on his own; and that's why age-mates are so valuable in human development. Adults

[31] Argyle, *op. cit.*, pp. 57–63.
[32] Dorothy Burlingham and Anna Freud, *Young Children in Wartime: A Year's Working Residential War Nursery* (London: Allen & Unwin, 1942).

tend to expect too much or too little, to be too critical or not critical enough. Peers and playmates, like one's siblings, have no compunction, but neither do they have impossible standards. They can come to justice, fairness, and the rules of the game in a rough-and-ready fashion. While children all reflect their parents' culture and parental conditioning, they also partake of a well-nigh universal juvenile subculture of play and exploration.[33] Certain children's games have been the same since ancient Egyptian culture, and probably before. Judging from all other cultures (and the evidence of primates), children have always had a need for each other's company and companionship. Juvenile relationships and juvenile games are an important preparation for adult relationships, adult work, and adult society.[34]

No parent can successfully protect his child from the testing of his peers. If a parent can fully control the situation, then the child isn't getting from his peers what he needs. Even the most pampered prince guaranteed a divine right to rule in adulthood would have to have experience with his equals in childhood in order to rule successfully. Our children, who do not inherit position and assured success, must much more learn to operate in relationships of equality. Or perhaps we should say in relationships of inequality, since children make no bones about individual differences. Learning about individual differences and learning to live with them are among the things a child learns from his playmates. But sometimes the lessons are too harsh, too cruel, too soon.

Thus a good parent encourages his child to engage in peer relationships but does not withdraw completely. As with sibling rivalry within the family, parents may have to protect by inter-

    [33] Iona and Peter Opie, *The Lore and Language of Schoolchildren* (Oxford: Clarendon Press, 1959).
    [34] Sherwood L. Washburn, "Aggressive Behavior and Human Evolution," *Social Change and Human Behavior, op. cit.,* "Adaptive Significance of Play," pp. 25–26.

vening directly. With neither prejudice nor "pathological even-handedness,"[35] parents exert parental influence. The parent and the family should remain strong, but the child should not be isolated. Every child needs many things that the family cannot give. He must be able to develop autonomy, mastery of the environment, his own self-direction and the fulfillment of his own talents. He must be able to solve problems and have the satisfactions of coping well in the environment outside the home. A child knows he must grow up and take his place in the world and he wants to do so competently.

Erik Erikson speaks, of the virtue of competency[36] which each child needs to develop. In our culture, school should be giving children a sense of competency. They want to learn to handle the tools, skills, and techniques of the adult world in preparation for joining the world. The self-confirmation that a child gets from being competent and being able to handle his work and training is all important. A good parent tries to ensure this development for his child and guard him from a sense of failure and frustration. A parent provides a back-up support system for the child's launching into the society. Part of this involves conscious briefings and instructions of all a parent's accumulated information and wisdom about coping with life, from sex to money to religion and politics. Parents pass on their culture consciously and make efforts to teach directly. They try to prepare their children for adulthood. Some failure, some frustration in learning to overcome obstacles is inevitable for each child, but hopefully the balance will be weighted with confidence and mastery.

A competent youngster with a positive self-image is able to face adolescence and a final weaning from dependence. Naturally there's a great deal of ambivalence in both parent and

[35] Henry, *op. cit.*, p. 33.
[36] Erik H. Erikson, *Insight and Responsibility* (New York: W. W. Norton, 1964), p. 129.

child upon the child's move beyond the parents' world, beyond dependency. Parents become consultants rather than controllers.[37] The transition will be different for every family, but usually the parent is presented with a delicate problem. How does a parent offer support, complete with contacts and financial help, when the ultimate goal of that support is separation? It's the parental problem in a nutshell. How do you raise a child well, so he will want to leave? It's an interesting paradox. Birds may push their young out of the nest, or other animals may simply desert the young at the appropriate time. Human parents must be more subtle in our confused, affluent American world. While some young people have to be slowed down in their mad rush for independence, other more timid types have to be nudged out of the nest. Usually it's a back-and-forth process. There's a growing trend among many adolescents toward lingering dependence.[38] When the young drop out of college in record numbers, they go home to live with indulgent parents.

But the break has to be made somewhere on the road to maturity. You can't go home again once you've really reached adulthood. If a child won't declare his independence, then parents have to declare theirs for the good of all concerned. A person has to leave father and mother emotionally in order to mature, marry, work, and produce a new generation of children. Parents have to have a life and purposes outside their children and vice versa. A good parent very skillfully and wisely works himself out of a job. You measure success by how little you are still needed in an adult child's life. Loved, yes; admired, yes; but needed, no. Good parenthood has a built-in disap-

---

[37] Gordon, *op. cit.*, pp. 275–77.

[38] Bruner asks the most disturbing question: "Is the functional prolongation of immaturity so great that transition to adulthood is interfered with by the strong establishment of immature response patterns? One can produce such effects in other species." Bruner, *op. cit.*, p. 18.

pearing dynamic; in the language of ecology, good parenting is biodegradable.

In a young adult establishing independent identity, there may be a period of definite withdrawal and separation from parents. Parents and adolescents tend to arouse old deep feelings in each other that are hard to handle.[39] A mobile culture like ours often accomplishes separation with distant travel or work. After maturity and independence have been thoroughly established, however, a new closeness with parents is possible and often develops. A young adult who is attempting to raise a family of his own reappreciates his parents. Parental strengths and failures are seen in a new perspective when one is oneself a parent. Good parents are appreciated in their old age by their children who are themselves mature; they can honor their parents with more understanding as they grow older.

With increasing longevity and health there is an interesting new stage of parenthood when both parents and children are mature adults fully functioning in society. Parents in youthful middle age and children in young adulthood provide a new dimension to parenthood. Full equality is possible for many parents and children in a new way. It's a time to savor; "ripeness is all." Good parents are then models of how to negotiate the transition to part-time and postparental stages of life,[40] no easy feat (especially for women in our culture). Little emphasis has been given to living in full maturity and having a successful middle age. Such a neglect of middle years is a prelude to the scandal of old age in America. Few parents can help but fear our culture's degrading dismissals of the old.

In the final years of parenthood the roles of parent and child are slowly reversed. An aged parent may find himself dependent

[39] E. James Anthony, "The Reactions of Parents to Adolescents and to Their Behavior," *Parenthood, op. cit.*, pp. 307–24.

[40] Therese Benedek, "Parenthood During the Life Cycle," *Parenthood, op. cit.*, pp. 185–206.

upon his adult children. In the seven ages of man the last is usually much like the first in helplessness. The parent is then child to his own child. The difficulty of this situation needs no elaboration. The final challenge of parenthood may be to learn to receive gracefully, to retire from a dominant position, and die with grace and dignity. Facing death with courage is a final legacy and example one can leave to one's children and grandchildren. Perhaps the final test of parenthood will be found in the behavior of one's children in old age. Quite often they give back to a parent what they received. Bitter harvests are not all confined to the world of drama; King Lear is not alone. Erik Erikson has observed that in old age a person is moved to make a final thrust toward personal integrity.[41] Restitution and reconciliation with one's own life are the final human tasks. Parents have this final growing forced upon them through the behavior and lives of their grown children.

In the end, as in the beginning, a parent succeeds through inculcating love and respect, the basis of parental authority. Imitation, identification, and modeling are the core of parent-child process.[42] A child naturally imitates his parents and if the parent is loving and good, the child will identify with him in deep and superficial ways. A child incorporates much of his parent's personality even if he hates it, but if he loves and admires his parent then the identification process is strengthened. The parents' marriage, their capacity to work and love are the media and the message. This process of identification is the primary form of learning and the most effective way values, lifestyle, and emotional attitudes are transmitted from parent to child. Whether we will, or no, we create our children

[41] Erikson, *op. cit.*, pp. 132–34.

[42] Jerome Kagan, "The Concept of Identification," and Albert Bandura and Aletha C. Huston, "Identification as a Process of Incidental Learning," *Readings in Child Development and Personality*, ed. by Paul Henry Mussen, John Janeway Conger, and Jerome Kagan (New York: Harper & Row, 1965), pp. 212–23, pp. 247–62.

present doubts about personal relationships. Even if someone grew up in such a community, chances are that by adulthood they have moved on to a new locality, a new class, a new lifestyle. Parents today, like everyone else, are perpetually assaulted with conflicting information, conflicting values, and other assorted anxiety-messages. The new media pound away with their complete coverage. Still one of the ways people get information and messages about values is through that original mass media, the printed word. Books are here to stay. Lives have been changed when an individual decides to take and read a book. So why not books to prepare for parenthood? They are read to learn from the insight and knowledge of others.

Turning to a parental guidebook implies a typically American desire to do better. Better than one has been doing, better than neighbors and kinfolk, or better than one's own parents. It's an optimistic belief in progress and faith that the future can be better than the past. Why should traditional errors, or even past inadequacies, be perpetuated in the name of filial piety? With a will to be good, and enough effort, Yankee faith asserts that parents can correct past mistakes and do a better job. Parents can make their children happier than they were themselves and at the same time make the world a better place. The nineteenth-century ideal of the Edenic home is still with us; home sweet home will produce people who will regenerate society. Who knows what lust for progress and perfectibility lurks in the hearts of Americans? It's not surprising that a guide such as Dr. Spock's book on baby and child care continually nudges the Bible on the best-seller lists, for more parents than ever have the faith. They believe that parenting can be improved, should be improved, and will be improved with informed effort. I think reading parents are right—for many reasons.

First of all, most parents can only find out about the work done in this century in child development through a popular book. The average reader of a how-to parent book is not going to be able to find his way through the texts of Montessori, Piaget, Gesell, Freud, Bowlby, Spitz, Erikson, Winnicott, Kohlberg, and the many other significant researchers in child development. If he did, the disagreements among theorists are so confusing that a good synthesis and popularization can serve a real need. Besides, many of the great foreign researchers need to have their work adapted to the American scene and updated. (The Geneva adolescents Piaget observed have a very different life from their American counterparts, just as the Freudian father was a nineteenth-century-European specialty.) All in all, I think parenting manuals can help to disseminate very important ideas.

From personal experience I can testify that despite an excellent education in the humanities, I never knew the importance of play and delight in a child's development until I read it in a parenting book. Coming across this new idea in a written form, I began to observe my young children more closely. When personal observation confirmed reading, I began to meet their needs for a better play environment. It had just never occurred to me that children could be bored and stultified at such a young age, or that providing pleasure could be so important in parenting. Getting new ideas through books can alert parents so that they can learn to see their children afresh and more creatively. They also learn what has been observed of many other children at the same ages. Parents are saved a lot of needless worry if they can share in the collective experience of other parents and children. Unfortunately, few modern parents have any extensive personal experience with caring for children. Until we have more communal living or family life courses complete with apprenticeships, books will serve the real needs of American parents.

Indeed, most of the popular parenting manuals, written since the Second World War, try to synthesize new knowledge in particularly American ways. Each of these popular books is founded on the assumption that parents are reading this book in order to raise successful children. Having *successful* children has always been important to Americans, either as a proof of their child's salvation (under the older religious regime) or as a justification of parental sacrifice and pride in their work for the cause of progress. There's always an ambiguous mixture of altruism, work ethic, and ego boosting when American parental psychology is analyzed. Either altruism or personal pride can raise self-consciousness and induce parental anxiety. Although parental anxiety could sell more how-to parent books—these books invariably start out reassuring parents. The optimistic line maintains that parents are more capable than they think they are; parents should relax.

Reassuring parents also manifests the traditional democratic suspicion of expert elites. The author-experts no longer claim to know all, or even to know better than parents; they just claim that they are masters of a special technology or science of child care which they wish to share. There is an Ame.`˙ ˙n belief in technology at work here. And better still, this particular scientific technology is built on common sense and actual experience. Since parents possess common sense and have experience with their own child, they are welcomed as fellow authorities and given a great deal of respect in popular parental guides. In one sense, parents are "in" at the moment—their decisions are given validity, and parental authority is championed. (Parents also buy the books, of course.)

Today, parental guilt is assuaged and parental mistakes are allowed. Who doesn't make mistakes? Humorous anecdotes of the author-expert's own parental mistakes are a regular feature of these books. Yet, despite lapses, we all, as fellow parents (goes the message), must keep on trying to be wise and keep on improving—at the same time we are enjoying our children and becoming more relaxed and spontaneous. Never has enjoyment and expertise been so linked with a technology, except perhaps in American sex manuals. Of course child-care experts also worry about their cheery advice being misused to justify parental neglect and abuse; so most authors cover their relaxed approach by including a section in which they give the signs and symptoms of *serious* parental malfunctioning. If any of the extreme conditions are present, then immediate expert help is advised. These lists of serious problems get the expert off the hook. Having disposed of the pathological fringe, they can continue to reassure parents as they go through the topics of parental concern—Discipline, Feeding, Developmental Timetables, etc. Like pediatricians in the practice of medicine, those who write books on child care have decided that parents are the real patients; they need help in order to help their child. True enough.

Therefore the most delicate task in all education has to be undertaken. The expert who really wants to be effective (just like the parent who wants to rear his child well) has to activate another. Parents have got to do the job on the spot all by themselves. Parents have to be built up and given confidence in their values and judgment at the same time that helpful advice, instruction, and new information are being conveyed to them, and harmful behavior discouraged. It's hard to do this through the printed word and no expert really handles this problem consistently. There's a great deal of going back and forth from reassurance to severe cautioning and authoritarian pronouncements. At issue is the question of parental certitude and confidence. Would you rather have parents who confidently make mistakes, sure of themselves as parents, or parents with enough self-doubt to take the expert's advice?

One author, Allan Fromme of *The ABC of Child Care*, states his position bluntly: "Although this volume is designed to give many of the answers, its effect on parents depends more on the sense of certainty it helps them develop than on the absolute accuracy of the information itself. In other words, knowledge of this sort is valuable only if it helps a person believe more than ever that what he is doing is correct."[1] In other words, better to have benevolent certainty than the truth. Characteristically, this same author, writing in the more authoritarian fifties, displays a lot of undoubting benevolent certainty in his own advice to parents. He tells parents to space your children from three and a half to five years, to avoid spanking, to discourage pacifiers, and he can begin an explanation of guilt with the self-confident phrase, "The way it all happens is as follows. . . ."[2]

He also maintains that what good parents have to know about heredity is "Nothing—absolutely nothing!"[3] He is sure that "Our child's personality and behavior have nothing directly to do with heredity."[4] Since parents are the dominant influences in a child's personality, difficulties with a child should be the cause of self-scrutiny: "The only reason we wonder sometimes how our children got to be the way they are, despite our good intentions, is that we don't understand ourselves as well as we like to think we do. To correct this, we unfortunately make the mistake of trying to understand the *children* better instead of trying to understand *ourselves* better."[5] Finally, another example of expert authority on display is the rule (naturally there are lots of rules and 1, 2, 3, solutions), "As always, it's better to do nothing at all than the wrong thing."[6]

Does such authoritarian advice make a parent confident and certain? I wonder. Commanding an audience to benevolent certainty may not produce the desired result, especially if you

1 Allan Fromme, *The ABC of Child Care* (Copyright, 1956, New York: Pocket Books, 1969), xiii.
2 *Ibid.*, p. 132.
3 *Ibid.*, p. 135.
4 *Ibid.*
5 *Ibid.*, p. 204.
6 *Ibid.*, p. 202.

give so many rules. If the parents submit to the expert's authority and rules, can they learn to exercise their own judgment? We find different approaches in the parent manuals which lead the best-seller lists in the seventies. Twenty years makes a difference. For simplicity's sake let's concentrate on the three superstars of popular child-rearing books: Dr. Haim G. Ginott of *Between Parent and Child* and *Between Parent and Teen-ager* (1969),[7] Dr. Fitzhugh Dodson of *How to Parent* (1970),[8] and the now revised and updated (1969) Dr. Benjamin Spock's *Baby and Child Care*.[9] There must be three hundred other popular books on child rearing and half again as many gurus, but these are among the most popular and omnipresent. (Other very important and popular figures are Dr. Lee Salk, Dr. Thomas Gordon and Dr. Bruno Bettelheim.) All represent the strengths and problems of the genre very well. With some references to the other experts and other books we can get a contemporary view of professional parenting advice in the seventies.

By now the attitude toward parents is modified and the authoritarianism of earlier how-to books is generally more subtle. There is an increasing sympathy for the parents in their increasingly more difficult task. As one perceptive expert says, parents are "blamed but not trained."[10] There's a recognition that while there's no societal recognition for being a good parent, it takes more constant personal effort than anything else in life. I agree. It is an ultimate challenge which is thoroughly ignored in all measurements of accomplishment and status.

[7] Dr. Haim G. Ginott, *Between Parent and Child* and *Between Parent and Teen-ager* (New York: Avon Books, 1971).

[8] Dr. Fitzhugh Dodson, *How to Parent* (New York: The New American Library, Inc., 1971).

[9] Dr. Benjamin Spock, New Revised and Enlarged Edition, *Baby and Child Care* (New York: Pocket Books, 1970).

[10] Dr. Thomas Gordon, *Parent Effectiveness Training* (New York: Peter H. Wyden, 1970), p. 1.

Most of the popular books on parenting recognize all the distractions and temptations that can make modern parents' task more difficult, including the fact that parenting is a daily "hidden" phenomenon. As Dr. Ginott says so well, "Parenthood is an endless series of small events, periodic conflicts, and sudden crises which call for a response. The response is not without consequence: It affects personality for better or for worse."[11]

The ambivalence such a demanding situation arouses in parents is also fully recognized. Parents reading guidebooks in the seventies know that experiencing fatigue, resentment, and difficulties are not their personal idiosyncratic responses to parenting. The joy, delight, pleasures, and satisfactions of parenting are also stressed more than ever (always on the back-cover blurbs), but inside there is the realistic recognition that parenting is hard, and sometimes harder than we ever expected. Therefore, parents need help from an expert who through expert advice helps share some of the burden and eases the psychological pressure. But the experts of the seventies don't avoid the nagging conflict of whether parents should trust more to expert information and skills or more to their own spontaneous emotional responses.

Dr. Spock, echoing his first editions in the forties, begins his book with the dictum, "Trust Yourself. . . . You know more than you think you do."[12] He continually urges parents to trust themselves and their common sense, for the experts have come to the conclusion that "what good mothers and fathers instinctively feel like doing for their babies is usually best after all."[13] Confident parents are best, and the more child-rearing theory you know, the more anxious and unsure you may become. He's sure that "it's a tougher job when you know the

11 Ginott, *op. cit.*, p. 243. (All quotes are from *Between Parent and Child* unless specified.)
12 Spock, *op. cit.*, p. 3.
13 *Ibid.*, p. 193.

theory."[14] Dr. Spock also carries this to the point of preferring confidence over everything, even when dealing with adolescents: "In most cases it's better to do the supposedly wrong thing with an air of confidence than the supposedly right thing with a hesitant or apologetic manner."[15] Benevolent certainty is still very much on the scene.

Dr. Dodson also thinks that in the crunch, parents should trust their hearts above theory. In an unsure situation, "Science may tell you one thing and your own heart may tell you something else. Believe your own heart! Common sense may tell you one thing and your own heart may tell you another. Believe your own heart!"[16] After a whole book detailing reams of advice, Dr. Dodson concludes that in a conflict love is more important than scientific information or even common sense. He and Dr. Spock agree that after all is said and done, instinctive parental feeling is the most trustworthy guide.

On the other hand, another popular mentor, Dr. Haim Ginott, is quite sure that "Love is not enough. Insight is insufficient. Good parents need skill."[17] Which methods we use in dealing with children will make a real difference. Love which is not communicated or is communicated in harmful ways will not be effective and may be counterproductive. Therefore, parents need to learn skills, particularly skills in communication. Ginott puts his emphasis upon verbal communication and so he ignores the medical aspects of child rearing and most preschool problems. Happily, he is interested in the more neglected school-aged child and the much analyzed teen-ager; he concentrates on the older child's relationship with his parents and with his teachers. In both cases common sense and instincts are not to be trusted over knowledge and skills. Dr.

14 *Ibid.*
15 *Ibid.*, p. 426.
16 Dodson, *op. cit.*, p. 232.
17 Ginott, *op. cit.*, Teen-ager, p. 243.

Thomas Gordon's book (and movement), *Parent Effectiveness Training,* also stresses educating small groups of parents in *skills.*[18]

Whom do we trust on the question of trusting parents' instincts? Of course, to be fair, each of these experts, and anyone conversant with the field (or life), always contends that the over-all and unique situation of parent and child is the most important thing in making any particular judgment. Each expert continually makes this point and continually stresses that with any serious problem there is no substitute for going to a pediatrician or seeking face-to-face professional guidance. But aside from the crisis situation there is still a difference in approach to parenthood. Is heart more important than head? Is too much knowledge of children and child-rearing theory dangerous for parents?

I would say no. I'll continue to defend how-to parent books, and the experts who synthesize and share their knowledge and experience. Those who contend that man is an intellectual reasoning being who is governed mainly by social learning have the better argument. I don't think there is any innate "parental instinct" or any "common sense" or even any "heart" which has not been socially learned. Also, unfortunately, parental instinct, common sense, and heart can all be wrong. Particularly when a culture such as ours is undergoing rapid change and is so unsatisfactory to so many of its members. We may need change in child-rearing practices when past instincts and common sense endorsed physical punishment, racism, social injustice, aggression, and apathy. Family breakdown, alcoholism, drug use, and child abuse increase and may be telling us something about the state of our hearts. When things are falling apart or changing, and parents are reading how-to books because they are searching for a better way, relying on a concept

18 Gordon, *op. cit.,* pp. 1–12.

of common sense (or the last decade's theories) will not do. Nor is heart enough or love enough. I would far rather parents trust their head and thereby be open to new information and the reasonableness of changing to better ways of doing things. The first parents who vaccinated against smallpox, stopped threatening their sons with castration, or gave up whipping children with belts may have gone against their instincts, their hearts and common sense. Instincts and common sense have a way of coinciding with the way one is brought up and what everybody else does.

The problem of trusting to either heart or head should, however, be distinguished from the question of self-confidence. I believe in trusting primarily to one's intelligence, head, and the best theory, but however you arrive at a decision, it *is* important to act confidently. You get this confidence from the fact that you are doing the best you know how to do. With it goes a healthy ability to tolerate a self-questioning which is open to improvement. A delicate balance of a lot of self-trust and a little self-distrust is needed in all of life's transactions, including parenthood. Living with some uncertainty, we can be open to a better way. But until we see a better way, we confidently continue. This is a good parent's qualified confidence, and semicertainty, the subtleties of which the guidebooks miss. They have confused the question of parental uncertainty with the problem of overanxious inconsistency, with its wide swings of parental moods and methods. Parents can calmly go their uncertain way pretty consistently and confidently, and still be questioning enough to listen and look for better solutions.

Indeed, even the most modern sensitive authors of how-to books are still semiauthoritarian. They have to be because they are trying to change parenting by showing parents a better way. They may not fully admit that they are trying to intervene and control parental behavior but, of course, they are. Why else write a book? Value judgments and theoretical assumptions appear on every page, and while some times they are recognized and labeled, often they are not. Dr. Spock, for instance, includes a whole section discussing the aims and values in child rearing, which is quite explicit in its endorsement of certain ideals and values—religion, patriotism, family, purposes beyond a child-centered home.[19] Those who blame Dr. Spock for a generation of rebelling spoiled kids should read it and repent of their accusations. (Or did Dr. Spock repent first and revise his ideas in reparation?) At any rate, Dr. Spock tries to make his own biases and assumptions explicit. Of course he has plenty left which are not recognized, and this is also true of most of the experts and their books. Basic theories of personality formation, issues which are being violently debated, are given forth without any reservations or qualms. For every doubt expressed, bias made explicit, or theoretical conflict recognized, two bold assertions can be found.

Now my complaint is not that how-to books are written, sides taken, or arguments pressed. I only argue that the theories presented and the underlying assumptions being made should be more explicitly given. More self-conscious and explicit explanations of their theories by experts would help how-to books. Otherwise, parents do not trust experts or follow them; nor can parents make informed choices between different kinds of advice. Answers to parental questions of why? and how do you know? are as important as answers to how-to questions; and such discussions of underlying assumptions can be put into popular, concise prose. In my opinion, how-to books can be ranked in quality and effectiveness by their success in explaining their own ground plans, goals, and implicit rules of the game. The troops may not follow the uncertain trumpet, but it's also important to know which war you're going to, before joining up. Why should a parent follow advice if he doesn't agree with the advisor's goals?

[19] Spock, *op. cit.*, pp. 10–17.

One of the very best books in its explicit explanations is Selma H. Fraiberg's *The Magic Years*,[20] subtitled *How to Understand and Handle the Problems of Childhood from Birth to School Age*. The emphasis is on helping parents *understand* the problems, and Fraiberg carries through on this claim admirably. She does so within a psychoanalytic theoretical framework which she carefully outlines and labels in the preface, thanking Anna Freud, René Spitz, Heinz Hartmann, and Ernst Kris. Her world view and her ideas about human nature are made explicit at the beginning of the book without a lot of professional jargon. She also confesses that although she follows a psychoanalytical-ego psychology, "The problems of child-rearing which we will deal with in these pages can only be dealt with on the level of our present knowledge, a psychology of the child which is large but incomplete in vital areas."[21] This was written in the late fifties (1959) but still sounds refreshing in its modesty. I don't agree with all of Fraiberg's theories but her non-authoritarian approach and recognition of the importance of theory is exemplary.

Fraiberg defends the existence of theories while discussing the changes in child-rearing theories during this century. She recognizes that parents have a right to be skeptical and says, "A theory is not, after all, a fashion. A scientific theory derives from observation. It is a valid theory when it passes rigid tests in use."[22] The theories in the twenties were poor theories in Fraiberg's opinion (and in my opinion, too) because they were not based upon a very large amount of observation and made assumptions regarding an infant's abilities which could hardly be proved, or even seem sensible. At any rate she defends theories in general and, in particular, theories which "derive from

[20] Selma H. Fraiberg, *The Magic Years* (New York: Charles Scribner's Sons, 1959).
[21] *Ibid.*, p. 31.
[22] *Ibid.*, p. 74.

an understanding of the developing child, of his physical and mental equipment at any given state and, therefore, his readiness at any given stage to adapt, to learn, to regulate his behavior according to parental expectations."[23] Fraiberg is of the school which holds that there is nothing quite so practical as a good theory. In child rearing her major over-all theory emphasizing child development and a child's changing needs as he grows makes immediate sense. Children need different things and are ready for new experiences as they develop.

Such an understanding of developmental stages in a child over time means that different principles of parenting will be applicable at different stages. A parent can change from a principle of total gratification of needs, appropriate in infancy, to the gradual frustrations needed in socialization, to the complete hands-off policy needed for young adult independence. There are different principles of parental adaptation at work, and even these principles will have to be varied in response to the unique child with unique parents in a unique life situation. Most difficulties arise, according to Fraiberg, at the points of transition in developmental stages, or when particularly stressful life events occur which present crises. Happily these ideas Fraiberg discusses so well have been accepted by all child-rearing experts. Almost every popular how-to book tries to get the message across; each child is unique and a wholistic approach within a developmental framework is the best approach. Dr. Dodson, for instance, makes this point by refusing to give an index to his book, in order to keep parents from looking up one isolated topic and thereby forgetting that the whole situation is important.

Despite variations and differences there is a fairly orthodox line in today's child-care books; we find a consistent synthesis which is worthy of praise. (More criticism later.) The present generation of parents and children are harvesting in our popu-

[23] *Ibid.*, p. 75.

lar manuals the fruits of much previous work. Perhaps we should begin by recognizing the accomplishments of the medical revolution in infant and child care which we usually take for granted. Although we may have problems with distributing health care and problems with doctor-patient communication and relationships, we still have an astounding amount of medical progress to be thankful for. Our children can be protected from an ever-increasing number of crippling diseases; diseases which in the past made survival in childhood problematical. This fact shapes our whole modern concept of parenthood; frequent mourning over lost children has been spared modern parents. Helplessness before the scourge of disease and death is not a routine part of our parental experience. Parental handbooks do not even have to provide medical advice since it is assumed that middle-class children will have access to pediatric medical care as a matter of course.

When medical advice is included in a how-to book, it can concentrate on preventive medicine, instructions for the rare emergency, and advice on when to call the doctor. Since no physician can prescribe by a book, not much more can be included beyond danger signals. One pediatrician with good sense and a humorous approach, Dr. Marvin Gersh, even includes a section on "How to Wean Yourself from Baby Books."[24] Dr. Gersh concludes that there is no substitute for parental experience in discerning when something is serious or not, and since doctors must neither give a false sense of security nor make parents too anxious, no book can be of too much help. With a good pediatrician and a little parental experience, the need for medical advice in book form disappears, except for emergencies.

Perhaps the most important medical advice in parent hand-

[24] Marvin J. Gersh, *How to Raise Children at Home in Your Spare Time* (New York: Stein & Day, 1966).

books are the chapters devoted to babyproofing the home and avoiding accidents. Ironically, we are in a situation in this country where more young children die from accidents than from disease. Parents and others engaged in child care could profitably memorize the poison, accident, and emergency chapters in handbooks. But for day-to-day living, parents really read how-to books, seeking advice on the handling of well children in order to ensure their continued health and well-being.

In questions of daily health care, there has been a general relaxation in medical theories of diet, feeding, sleep, and exercise out of doors. The rigid schedules and diets of the thirties have been replaced by a more child-centered approach. Instead of forcing children to eat, sleep, and exercise on rigid programs, today there is more emphasis upon self-regulation. Realizing that different children may need different amounts of food and sleep, pediatricians try to cut down on coercion and reduce the resulting conflicts and anxieties in parents and children. While there are still differences between experts over the value of breast feeding in infancy, at least there is a general consensus that feeding should be a natural pleasant affair. Eating should be a pleasure rather than a medical therapy.

Today's child-rearing experts base their child-care advice upon a natural easygoing approach which aims at gradual self-regulation and gradual conformity of the child to the rest of the family's habits. As Dr. Gersh puts it: "The point of the matter is that a healthy child will regulate his own diet quite well. No child will starve to death if he is left alone. . . . LET US ALL RELAX."[25] And Dr. Dodson in explaining all the harm that can be done by withholding food or provoking unnecessary conflicts says: "After all, parents have a great biological ally in feeding their children: the child's own hunger. If we respect our child's individuality and see that this biological

[25] *Ibid.*, p. 49.

need is met we should have no feeding problems."[26] Ditto for Dr. Spock and others.

Parental relaxation depends on accepting the idea of "a great biological ally" within the child, combined with a new respect for each child's individuality. All the anxious mothers ready to stuff, smother, swaddle, and coerce infants and children have been called off by an appeal to nature. The idea that a child naturally wants to fulfill and regulate his needs for food, sleep, and exercise can be liberating to parents who may have felt totally responsible for a blank organism, the original tabula rasa.

Other parents may have been even more pessimistic, feeling that they had to coerce a child who in its inherent bent to evil and self-destruction would refuse to eat and sleep out of spite or rebellious will. Positing an innate drive toward health helps reduce parental anxiety over their role. But there is some question whether the anxious hovering mother one finds pictured in baby books is still the reigning American model. Some experts might claim that relaxation has already gone to an extreme. The rumblings of the nutrition experts and the allied health food movement indicting American eating habits are not yet reflected in the how-to books. It will probably take until the eighties before we get discussions of tiger's milk, brown rice, and enriched diets.

I'd also say that our national concerns about America's inactive lazy non-habits of exercise have not penetrated very deeply into parental handbooks. The work of Gesell on stages and ages of physical development is included, but exercise for health's sake is not given as much space as the psychological aspects of play and toys. Perhaps child experts and harassed pediatricians feel that they can leave something for the schools to worry about. But if parents don't feel the need to be con-

[26] Dodson, *op. cit.*, p. 44.

cerned about physical fitness from the beginning, for its own sake, then schools will not. If we do not want the human foot to atrophy in record time, or our adult death rates to counter our gains in infant and child mortality, then I expect more emphasis on exercise and fitness in future how-to books. The fitness movement will progress from executives (jogging and squash) to women (yoga for beauty) to children and child-care books. Are Canadian Royal Exercises for babies coming up?

Yet it is still easier for popular how-to books to synthesize the different theories of physical-health care than it is to agree on a psychological theory. When we come to the psychological side of child development and behavior control, there's a wider range of theoretical differences. A popular presentation has to achieve a delicate balance between different schools of thought. A mainstream central synthesis is usually attempted in our present popular books and although the results are a bit ragged, it's generally an admirable compromise. To get a new viable orthodoxy, two fairly recent extremes in theory have to be avoided, while a few important new movements are incorporated. Today's expert has to avoid the behavioristic dogma of the twenties, avoid the pop-Freudian permissiveness of the forties and incorporate new theories stressing the child's early intellectual development and inherited temperamental differences. A good synthesis is made more difficult, because the expert himself has been educated in one tradition or another and so finds it hard to be objective.

A child-care expert formed in a psychoanalytic tradition, for instance, finds it difficult to emphasize a small child's cognitive development. Emotional interaction seems so much more important, and the unconscious so much stronger than intellectual cognition and exploration of the world. A theorist who has been taught that parental attitudes and handling mostly determine a child's temperament finds discussion of different inherited temperaments doubtful. Every expert is challenged to keep up with new findings, overcome his own biases, and take the best from all the theories in order to meld them into advice which can really help parents and children.

Perhaps it's easiest to avoid the behavioristic rigidity of the twenties and thirties. During that period, there was a curious amalgam of ideas about children and parents which glorified regularity, schedules, strictness, and the principles of conditioning. Stamping in good habits was all important. People were sure that infants could be "spoiled" by fondling, feeding, and play at inappropriate times. Parents were encouraged to do their duty and resist "giving into" children and thereby ruining their character. The underlying assumption, of course, was that parents were completely responsible for how their children turned out. Parental teaching and infant learning were the sole determiners of development. Children were thought to learn language and everything else purely by imitation, conditioning, and reward. The founder of behaviorism, J. B. Watson, made the statement that sets an all-time record for authoritarian self-confidence:

> Give me a dozen healthy infants, well formed, and my own specified world to bring them up in, and I'll guarantee to take anyone at random and train him to become any type of specialist I might select—doctor, lawyer, artist, merchant-chief, and yes, even beggarman and thief, regardless of his talents, penchants, tendencies, abilities, vocations and race of his ancestors.[27]

Watson never doubted that his findings in laboratory experiments with animals could be applied to children. Behaviorism

[27] John B. Watson, *Behaviorism* (Chicago: University of Chicago Press, 1963, Copyright 1924), p. 104.

was a very "scientific" method, but in its own way, it was just as repressive and chilly in tone as the earlier puritan methods devised for breaking children's wills and reducing the effects of original sin. A close reading of Watson's work reveals that when he talks about "infantile" behavior, he means bad behavior which needs to be changed, without benefit of any biological ally within. Watson's concern for control and achievement is also puritanical in tone.

Although Watson proclaimed corporal punishment an unscientific method, he had this to say about the all-important need to "build in negative responses": "I thoroughly believe in rapping a child's fingers when it puts them in its mouth, when it constantly fingers its sex organs, when it reaches up and pulls down glass dishes and trays, or turns on gas cocks or water hydrants, etc., provided the child is caught in the act and the parent can administer the rap at once in a thoroughly objective way—just as objectively as the behaviorist administers the faint electric shock when building up a negative or withdrawal response to any given object."[28] Watson goes on to say how he would like to devise electrical shocks in forbidden things like table tops so the punishments would be objective. (Was this written before Huxley's *Brave New World* with its depiction of babies being shocked?)

The "objectivity" which appears in some of Watson's experiments is indeed chilling. One particularly painful experiment to read is one on "jealousy." The parents send their child off for a month to separate from the child; on his return they make affectionate love in front of the child, and when that fails to provoke him, they begin to attack each other. The mutual parental attacks and simulated crying finally cause the child to attack and become so "genuinely disturbed that the experiment had to be discontinued."[29] Some experiment! With scientists

28 *Ibid.,* p. 184.
29 *Ibid.,* p. 190.

as objective as Watson giving out theories and advice, the children of America were in trouble.

Although Watson gave up psychology and went into advertising, behaviorism and investigations in conditioned-learning theory kept on being developed. The most famous exponent of the school today is B. F. Skinner, who is of course nationally famous. When Skinner first became a parent several decades ago, he invented the famous Skinner Baby-Box, built to provide an environment for his child, which minimized germs, and cleaning chores. While rearing this same baby, Skinner came to believe in the uselessness of punishment. According to Skinner there are two versions of the story.[30] His daughter claims *she* told her parents to stop punishing her since it didn't do any good, but the parents think it was their own idea. There's always been a suspicion that children bring up parents, as well as vice versa, but it's difficult to prove your claim. Perhaps the testimony of another giant in the science of behavior, Neale Miller, is appropriate. He claims in a published interview that he made no special effort to apply the principles of his learning theories in raising his family because,

I'm sure the general principles do apply, but in my opinion we just don't have a science of child-rearing yet. There's too much ignorance about the important variables to go into human engineering with any confidence. In fact, my children taught me more about the complexities of human motivation than anything I taught them.[31]

These remarks provoke thoughts of all the children of psychologists who have taught their parents a few things. Piaget's children, Skinner's baby, Watson's poor little B, all the way

[30] Personal communication in lighthearted chat.
[31] Gerald Jonas, "Profile" article on Neale Miller, the *New Yorker* (August 19 and 26, 1972).

back to the children of Tiedemann (1787), and Pestalozzi in the nineteenth century. How many countless others have started their parents to thinking. This fact may have provoked a remark by the famous psychologist Allport to his student who had just become a father, "Marvelous, Brewster, every psychologist should have a child and a dog."[32]

Of course, when it comes to the behaviorists and learning theory, many might feel that the dogs had won the day. Most of these learning theorists would follow Watson and Skinner in not differentiating too much between training animals and training children. But today's popular parental handbooks do not fall into the "children-are-just-like-puppies fallacy."[33] Erikson's reminder that "dogs," unlike children, "are trained to serve and die"[34] is well taken. When learning principles which depend upon conditioning and rewards are recommended, they are incorporated with the idea that children can reason and love. All experts now agree that the most important thing a child must learn to have is a positive self-concept. So the other forms of human learning through insight, imitation, and identification with beloved parents are included in any discussion of learning laws culled from rats and pigeons. Dr. Dodson makes this explicit when he says that "there are psychological principles of teaching and learning which apply equally well to both animals and people . . . but there are other psychological principles of learning which apply specifically to human beings, and it behooves us parents to be familiar with these also."[35]

Even when the principles derived from animal learning are

[32] M. Brewster Smith, "Autobiographies: Three Psychologists and How They Grew," *Psychology Today*, Vol. 6 (September 1972), p. 67.

[33] An exception is *Ice Cream, Poker Chips, and Very Goods: A Behavior Modification Manual for Parents* by David L. Williams and Elliot B. Jaffa (Distributed by The Maryland Book Exchange, College Park, Maryland). Here are directions for modifying behavior with strict behaviorist principles.

[34] Erik H. Erikson, *Childhood and Society*, 2d. ed. (New York: W. W. Norton, 1963).

[35] Dodson, *op. cit.*, p. 236.

being used with children, there is a vast difference in the concept of reward. Instead of food pellets, the normal human child is rewarded by smiles, praise, and encouragement. In other words, you have to have a distinctly human relationship going. Fortunately, punishment is even out with animal training these days, except as a last resort. The preferred method of extinguishing undesirable traits is non-reward, or not noticing, a method which seems to apply to children too. Paying too much attention to undesirable behavior just reinforces it. Instead you must reward immediately for the smallest step toward the final goal.[36] By making initial successes possible, the prospective learner has a positive attraction to learning and less fear of failure. Naturally, the learner has to be able and ready to learn what you want to teach. As Dr. Dodson says, "Can you teach a dolphin to type?"[37]

Making accurate judgments about children's readiness and abilities is most important when it comes to teaching children. The genius of a Maria Montessori was not only that she discovered all of the above learning principles without recourse to rats and pigeons, but that she could expect more than others from supposedly retarded slum children. She also understood sophisticated principles of managing the environment in order to let the situation and materials teach a child, as well as understanding how to translate learning principles into concrete techniques appropriate for children. Breaking a task down into its component parts in order to better teach it, is one of the basic educational truths. Anyone who ever tried to teach a child to tie his shoelaces or wash his hands with soap understands the helpfulness of knowing the principles of learning.

When it comes to that particularly human learning task called self-discipline, popular how-to books have done a good

[36] *Ibid.*, pp. 203–16.
[37] *Ibid.*

job in correcting past inadequacies. They have avoided the rigidity of the twenties' habit-machine model and the looseness of the popular Freudian permissiveness that set in as a reaction in the forties. It's hard to imagine how permissive theories of child rearing were ever deduced from Freud's own work. But Americans have transformed many things on a transatlantic crossing. Freudianism, in its most popular misunderstood version, held that any parental frustration and inhibition of the child's impulses would be harmful. The fear was not of "spoiling" but of "traumatizing" the child with repression. Many parents, following this line of least resistance, abdicated their responsibility to socialize their children and some monstrously spoiled brats resulted. While there have always been American children who were not socialized by their parents, some of whom were also overindulged, in pop Freudianism there was a difference. Misunderstood Freudian permissiveness emphasized sexual freedom from repression as well as the inevitability of aggressive behavior. Consequently, a Freudian-spoiled brat was a much more anxious and sexually disturbed model than previous children whom parents had ignored or bribed. When parents almost encourage out-of-bounds behavior, it's most upsetting to a child. Parental permissiveness toward aggression and sexuality can be particularly scary.

Today all misunderstanding about the child's need for inhibition and parental control has been cleared up. Freud's real and very pessimistic and unpermissive views of life have been understood. It's now thought that if a child is first controlled by beloved parents, he can gradually develop his own internal controls as he matures and identifies with his parents.[38] If the parents never control him, or inhibit any behavior, or at the opposite extreme never give him any freedom to control himself, the child's development toward self-direction and self-

[38] Fraiberg, *op. cit.*, pp. 146–58.

control will be hampered. Through modeling himself on his parents a child learns to behave as his parents behave.[39] But the parents have to help the child in this process by controlling his environment and prohibiting dangerous and undesirable actions. Clearly and fairly consistently, the parents' "no" and external control eventually becomes the child's own "no" to himself and self-control.

Another distinction made in every popular how-to book today is the difference between feelings and actions. Every child-rearing expert warns parents not to try to repress and control a child's feelings, just his unacceptable behavior. The theory is that all kinds of acceptable and unacceptable feelings will inevitably come into the consciousness, and it's vitally important to admit and recognize what one feels without too much censorship. Verbal expression of one's real feelings will keep them from being bottled up and finally exploding. (This is applied to parents as well as children.) When people lose touch with the truth of their internal state, by being forced to deny and repress unacceptable feelings, they can no longer operate as a whole person. They may lose touch with their good feelings too. Therefore parents should encourage verbal expressions of feelings (ventilations of feeling), while forbidding and controlling harmful actions. Today's parental guidebooks are filled with techniques to enable parents and children to express their feelings and have them accepted as a valid experience. People are only responsible for their actions, not their emotions.

Personally, I am not so sure that feelings can get bottled up and cause psychic harm later. (They may simply fade away.) However, a theory which tries to avoid harmful repression is as good as any other and has many advantages. It encourages parents and children to be honest, to communicate more, and not worry about pleasing other people. Having the guts to speak up may be more therapeutic to self-esteem than ventilat-

[39] Dodson, *op. cit.*, pp. 213–54.

ing feelings supposedly is to psychic health. Also this theory of permitting negative feelings but forbidding harmful acts discourages and lessens the number of parental judgments and punishments—always a good thing. But finally it keeps the Pollyanna syndrome under control; parents are allowed to express their own weaknesses, too.

But parental weaknesses are more dangerous in parent-child relationships because the parents are so powerful and important to the child. Parental rejections, hurts, lapses, attacks, are felt with fourfold impact. Parents who harshly or continually punish, scold, or shame, turn the child against them and provoke hatred and rebellion toward everything and everyone else. For this reason most of the popular how-to books agree on deploring physical punishment, because it is humiliating and too severe. Physical constraint can curb aggression and physical isolation can deprive a child when he has misbehaved, but physically hurting a child is believed to be counterproductive. However, Dr. Spock and Dr. Dodson are exceptions who both think that a few parental swats on the backside can be better for both parent and child than other punishing techniques. Parents who induce guilt, verbally abuse, reject with irritability, or withdraw coldly may be more cruel than the occasional swatter. Both doctors also agree that a spank in anger is far better for parent and child than an inhumane spanking in cold objectivity. The idea is that a child can understand and forgive parental anger more easily than deliberate calculated hurting (à la Dr. Watson). The battle over physical punishment almost equals the controversies over whether to nurse or bottle-feed infants.

Personally, I think the how-to books which put a tabu on spanking are better for parents and children. In our violent culture, filled with pressures to be quick on the trigger, I think most parents abuse physical punishment if they use it at all. Violent behavior has a built-in demonic dynamic which tends to escalate; most parents are too vulnerable and under too much stress to even countenance spanking. If we did not have a horrible national history of violence toward children at home and school and did not live in a time of growing child abuse, we might give more leeway to the occasional spanking. But at present the hitting habit should be erased from home and school in the name of justice. Hitting hurts. Shaking a child may even cause whiplash and brain injury. The most severe physical punishment I would countenance would be the salutory shoulder grip and squeeze, a face-to-face, eye-to-eye, hands-to-shoulder punctuation of a verbal message. A child cannot squeeze-grip an adult back or even hurt a smaller child if he imitates your parental loss of temper (which he will). In the long run, cultural tabus on some things like spanking are better than making exceptions.

But parents do have rights. Parents have to have their self-respect and their own lives. (It's important for the child to understand he is not the center of the world.) Without their own lives in a good state, the individuals who are parenting can't do as good a job. Even so, parents will inevitably display weakness and fallibility and from this a child learns a hard lesson. People are not perfect and neither is the world. In an imperfect world, unpleasant things like discipline, social standards, and self-control are necessary in order to live with others. Parents have to raise a child who can live with others in the real world, and the best way to do so is to assert a parental right to live while parenting. Every how-to book for parents stresses that parents need their own interests, both as individuals and as a married couple in order to do a good job.

It is agreed. The total adaptation of parents to infants "find out what the baby wants and then give it to him"[40] must

[40] Donald W. Winnicott, "The Mother-Infant Experience of Mutuality," *Parenthood*, E. James Anthony and Therese Benedek, eds. (Boston: Little, Brown & Co., 1970), pp. 245–56.

gradually give way to separation and independence of parents and children from each other. In a curious way some parents can be too good, too wonderful. (As if parents didn't have enough problems!) As Abraham Maslow, the psychologist who specialized in analyzing self-actualizing people, puts it: "Bad parents create certain problems, but wonderful parents also create certain problems which may be different, but which are still problems."[41] The point is that superior, strong, intelligent, talented, loving people may be overwhelming to their children; children faced with all of that strength may give up hope and sink in feelings of inferiority. This is sadly unsettling, says Maslow, "because everybody a priori expects that wonderful people will make wonderful parents and that wonderful parents will make wonderful children. Point out that it's not so good for kids to have wonderful parents."[42] This point reiterates the complexity of the parenting process. Activating another human being requires self-restraint and a certain passivity and absencing to allow growing room. An analogy from the religious realm comes to mind: Christ tells his followers that he must leave them in order for them to receive the Holy Spirit. To come of age (as disciple, psychoanalytic patient, or child) requires independence and initiative, some separation from the most wonderful of parental figures. Otherwise the child will never obtain full functioning in the larger world outside.

Indeed my main reservations about popular how-to books hinge on their view of the family's relationship to the world outside. The limited social horizon in how-to books also affects their view of sex roles within the family. Specialists in communication recognize that a lot more is communicated in a medium (such as how-to books) than is explicitly stated. As

---

[41] Abraham H. Maslow, *Eupsychian Management: A Journal* (Homewood, Illinois: Richard D. Irwin, and the Dorsey Press, 1965), p. 149.
[42] *Ibid.*

one expert who has studied the influences of different communication messages on attitudes shrewdly puts it:

> The most profound effects of communication can be found not in making sales, getting votes, influencing opinions and changing attitudes, but in the selective maintenance of relatively stable structures of images and associations that stem from institutional structures and policies and that define the common perspectives of a society.[43]

In other words, the pictures of life given in popular how-to books and the things they take for granted may be as influential as the advice.

The "stable structures of images" in Dr. Spock's book may be its biggest message. But all the popular parental guidebooks reflect the individualism, privatism, and sexism of American society. There is little recognition of alternate lifestyles, no consciousness of cross-cultural variations, or even any class or ethnic differences within America. These are mainstream, middle-class, white-oriented books with even our religious values hardly touched upon. The aesthetic dimension of life is also a bit scanted, although the rising consciousness of the importance of early intellectual development does penetrate. There's a persistent overconcentration upon early stages of child development (and early parenthood), so not enough is said about broader cultural education. Any idea of the political and social context in which parents raise children is totally absent. Nothing is said about urban versus suburban living or the special situation of living in a rural setting. How to get children involved in the community, and instill a sense of larger social and cultural purposes, is ignored.

Parenting is always seen as a private concern focused within

[43] George Gerbner, "Communication and Social Environment," *Scientific American*, Vol. 227 (September 1972), p. 158.

the four walls of the private utopian home. Within these walls, separated from the rest of the world, live the individuals who must relate to each other in the family. If standards of parental perfectibility have eased up a bit, while standards of permissiveness have tightened up and children are no longer seen as products of conditioning and instincts, still the isolated individualism of each family on its own is very much with us. The community may impinge on the family but mostly this is seen as a problem of TV in the home, not parents and children enmeshed in their community's struggles or purposes. As we saw above, Dr. Spock may present a short section on the need for values and larger purposes and goals, but the whole rest of the book is built on the assumption of the isolated home cut off from the rest of society. The assumption of a parental monopoly on child rearing is almost total. Grandparents appear and baby-sitters put in an appearance and schools and peers are discussed, but these are all bit players in the periphery of the ongoing drama of the private family life.

This particular American isolationism becomes particularly apparent when one reads a study like Urie Bronfenbrenner's *Two Worlds of Childhood: U.S. and U.S.S.R.*[44] In Bronfenbrenner's description of Soviet society and upbringing, with side looks at the kibbutz, he points out their great collective concern for rearing children. Their children's experience from the beginning is a great deal of interaction with peers, adolescents, and adults beyond the family. The aim and practice of Soviet child rearing is to have the child become a part of the larger society and feel responsible for it. Bronfenbrenner cites advice found in Soviet how-to-rear-children guides which apparently are widely read by parents, teachers, and the general public. As he says, "upbringing is virtually a national hobby

[44] Urie Bronfenbrenner, *Two Worlds of Childhood: U.S. and U.S.S.R.* (New York: Russell Sage Foundation, 1970).

in the U.S.S.R."[45] The whole society is nurturing toward children, most adults are deeply concerned and emotionally responsive to all children. Bronfenbrenner calls this a "diffusion of maternal responsibility"[46] in Soviet society.

In Bronfenbrenner's view, the society's collective responsibility and the idealistic goals that Soviet children embrace in the school and community help family life and the development of the individual child. Soviet society has many terrible flaws but in its treatment of children and in the organization of family life they have many strengths lacking in our own society. (Indeed many other countries and cultures are ahead of the United States in this respect.) The United States is singularly unsupportive of parents, teachers, or family life. Adult-child contact is minimal when there is an indifference to children and age segregation. This individualism and isolationism detailed in Bronfenbrenner's chilling chapter called "The Unmaking of the American Child," is perfectly mirrored in our how-to books. And it is not just our U.S. resistance to state interference and communism that is behind our lack of co-operative support. There is not a word, for instance, in a how-to book of a private family co-operating with another family in child rearing. It's every man for himself, every family for itself.

Even when schools, nursery or otherwise, enter into how-to books, the emphasis is upon the school and the individual child, never a discussion of parents co-operating with fellow parents or children working with children. No discussion appears of how the competitive structuring of schools affects children. The idea that parents might have to change the school to affect their child's welfare is completely absent. Competition may not be stressed in American child rearing as much

[45] *Ibid.*, p. 11.
[46] *Ibid.*, p. 8.

as it once was, but ideals of communal co-operation have certainly not come upon the scene.

Even in Ginott's books which stress the need for developing skills in communication with children, it's still assumed that adjustment to the status quo is important for the individual child's success. The image maintained is that of the isolated individual parent talking to the isolated individual child who must go back to the wars and win. As in the psychoanalytic model the one-to-one-talk-cure approach is presented; problems are within the child, or within the parents, and adjustment to the outside world is a private matter. While the parent is encouraged to be the advocate of the child, giving emotional support, he is not often enjoined to band together with other parents or actually investigate the objective situation with an eye to changing it. In other words horizontal relationships within the larger community are mostly non-existent; political social dimensions are ignored in favor of subjective private solutions and adjustments.

Also, in most parental how-to books there's but minimal recognition of the whole family as a system. The "family-point-of-view" is missing, that is, an understanding of the family as a whole unit greater than the sum of its parts.[47] The family therapy movement is founded on the premise that a family unit is a dynamic system in which each member has interpersonal interactions with every other individual in the family system. A family can be seen as an intricate organism with mutually interdependent members involved in dynamic relationships which tend to balance and homeostasis. Change in the interpersonal interactions within the family will change each individual, and vice versa. Such a systematic view of the family as a whole is foreign to the reigning individualism of

[47] Carlfred B. Broderick, *"Beyond the Five Conceptual Frameworks: A Decade of Development in Family Theory," Journal of Marriage and the Family,* Vol. 33 (February 1971), pp. 139–59.

America. Indeed, even a couple-oriented point of view is rare. Almost all parental how-to books are addressed to the mother alone.

The presumptions of isolated privacy in child rearing correlate perfectly with the pervasive sexism. These mostly masculine authors adhere (to a man) to theories of the Freudian family romance, the deep difference between boys and girls, and the assumption that mothers should have full-time care of the children. Working mothers are more or less ignored and discouraged, while fathers are thought to have a quite different and distinct role to play in raising their children. From reading these parental guidebooks, you could get the idea that nineteenth-century sex roles were still in force in the society. Anatomy is destiny and Nature rules; the women's liberation movement never happened. Day-care is also never mentioned, except in a few references here and there on the importance of individual care. It's no surprise, given this patriarchal world view, that penis envy is seen as a problem for little girls.

The flavor of these sections can be given: Dr. Dodson puts it on the line: "Let's face it: little girls feel somewhat deprived, and envious of boys";[48] or in Dr. Spock, "A little girl needs extra reassurance because it's natural for her to want to have something that she can see."[49] My favorite is Dr. Ginott's projected parent-daughter dialogue, "Sometimes girls have scary thoughts when they see that they don't have a penis. Do you sometimes wonder about that?"[50] These gentlemen don't seem to worry as much about womb envy among little boys, but they have very sure solutions for little-girl problems. A girl should be assured that she is not like her brother but is very different; she will be able to have babies when she grows up. As Dr. Spock outlines the parent-child strategy: "Then

[48] Dodson, *op. cit.*, p. 176.
[49] Spock, *op. cit.*, p. 371.
[50] Ginott, *op. cit.*, p. 182.

you try to make it clear, in a matter-of-fact cheerful tone, that girls and women are *made* differently from boys and men; they are *meant* to be that way."[51] Of course this difference (thought to create so much anxiety and castration fears) could be explained by saying that men and boys are made different from women, but the age-old assumption that man is the model of a human being and women are the different ones, still operates.

In the sexist world view, women are not made differently for variety's sake or for sexual pleasure, or for the glory of God; women are made "different" in order to be wives and mothers when they grow up. Mothers are very different from fathers in this universe. Mothers go through the "equivalent of an operation"[52] in childbirth, are subject to all sorts of disturbing glandular changes and of course, "In a majority of cases a woman's feelings are nearer the surface than a man's, more keenly felt."[53] A father's role in parenting is to give assurance and help, but, of course, not to give equal care to the baby, or the same kind of care. Fathers have to get in there for the sake of their boys, with masculine roughhousing and play, although according to Dr. Dodson, "At the same time he can display the tenderness and softness his little girl needs to encourage her coquettishness and femininity."[54] And Dr. Dodson is an expert who keeps telling parents not to be too rigid in sex stereotyping!

When you get to Dr. Ginott, you get the full biological-determinism package. He provides warnings to fathers who might take too much part in mothering activities such as feeding, diapering, and bathing the baby: "There is the danger that the baby may end up with two mothers, rather than with a

[51] Spock, *op. cit.*, p. 371.
[52] *Ibid.*, p. 30.
[53] *Ibid.*
[54] Dodson, *op. cit.*, p. 179.

mother and a father."[55] Why feeding, diapering, and bathing are essentially mothering activities is not made clear, it's just assumed to be natural, since it's traditional. Dr. Ginott has very strong ideas about a father's role and the importance of masculinity; fathers must be masculine in order to protect a child from his own wishes, from the outside world, and from his overprotective mother. Father is the traditional link to the outside world; while mothers may venture out, they are really supposed to find fulfillment at home.

Thus Dr. Ginott advises parents to teach girls the culinary and domestic arts and encourage boys to be more assertive and adventurous. "Boys will be boys" is an approved slogan in these books. Women in the family must appreciate the joys of homemaking or else the "girls in such homes may become competitive and feel compelled to outdo the boys, and later the men, at their own game."[56] Dreadful thought! Girls should be discouraged from competing and being assertive. Women are the natural nurturers, men the natural protectors and aggressive providers, so children should be prepared for these "natural" roles from childhood on. When the emphasis is upon the differences between the sexes, it follows that social-sexual roles will be different too. If you want to insure that the patriarchal status quo is maintained, there's no better place to begin than in telling parents to prepare girls for housekeeping and boys for aggressive achievement.

I think a far better way to insure self-acceptance of sexuality is through emphasizing physical integrity and individual personhood. Respect for one's own body and delight in sexual identity does not have to be tied to heterosexual gamesmanship (especially feminine coquettishness) or to reproduction. I would also maintain that parenthood is a mutual male and female process with equal privileges and responsibilities. Once

[55] Ginott, *op. cit.*, p. 201.
[56] *Ibid.*, p. 208.

beyond birth and nursing there is no special male or female sex-role function. "The overlap in behavior between the sexes," say some experts, "and human malleability is so great that both sexes are capable of exhibiting most forms of human behavior."[57] Two mothers, or two fathers, as two parents may do the same things for the child; protecting, loving, and preparing his way into the adult world. Parenting among humans does not have to be rigidly sex stereotyped and differentiated; nor does mothering have to be connected to housekeeping or fathering to breadwinning. Both parents can share these secondary functions just as they share the primary parenting.

It is a disservice to today's parents to encourage them to emphasize sex differences appropriate to yesterday's lifestyles when their children will grow up and live very different roles tomorrow. As one expert opinion on the development of sex and identity has it: "It is possible that the modern trend toward decreasing the severity of sex-role socialization occurs because it is being made subordinate to the more important rigors of raising a child to function from an early age in this symbolically complex culture."[58] With more complexity women and men are going to be sharing careers, parenting, and homemaking equally. They both need to be adept in instrumental and expressive roles, working and loving. Individual temperamental differences and individual competencies will be more decisive than sex differences. In other words, future how-to books are going to have to overcome all sexism and really be addressed to both parents, with more than token nods to father's parenting and women's work.

The present uneasiness that most how-to books reflect toward a working mother will be eased when the father's com-

---

[57] B. G. Rosenberg and Brian Sutton-Smith, *Sex and Identity* (New York: Holt, Rinehart & Winston, 1972), p. 88.

[58] *Ibid.*, p. 83. *cf.* also Philip E. Slater, "Parental Role Differentiation," *The Family: Its Structure and Functions* (Rose Laub Coser, ed. New York: St. Martin's Press, 1964), pp. 350–69.

mitment to child-care can be counted on. With fathers in the picture, and with communal co-operation and day-care on the scene, the experts need not be so worried about the young child getting enough consistent, loving individualized care. Indeed, when mothers have a life outside the family as well as within, then these same experts need not worry so much about maternal overprotection. A father will not have to protect his child from the mother's overprotection, when fathers and mothers are not raised so differently and do not function in such a polarized fashion.

But one thing will remain true in the future; having two parents will be an advantage. With two parents each can protect the child from the other, give each other support and provide a two-dimensional view on everything (along with the economic advantage). It's also important to learn early how to love members of both sexes and hopefully see a mutually satisfactory heterosexual relationship in operation. A strong couple relationship frees the child to grow up and leave parents who have each other, as well as it provides a model for his own mating.

But, I don't think a rigid Freudian version of the family romance operates in the ways that it may have in more patriarchal times. There are more complicated crossovers in love, attraction, and identifications in a family than originally outlined. Who possesses power, access to resources, competence, and what personality may be as big a factor in childhood identifications as Oedipus sexual dynamics. Most assuredly the child's development of conscience is not solely dependent upon the vicissitudes of the family romance. Many, many other factors enter into a child's development; yes, Virginia, even events that take place after six years old, outside of the family circle. Alas, very few popular how-to books are free from Freudian orthodoxy.

One refreshing maverick is found in Marvin J. Gersh's *How*

to Raise Children at Home in Your Spare Time.[59] Dr. Gersh
may direct his remarks mostly to mothers who possess "natural
feminine receptivity," but he can talk of the Oedipus complex
as an "American myth." He also allows as how parents are not
as important as they think. Dr. Gersh doesn't think early
childhood is decisive or that "sexual behavior is necessarily connected with the character of a person, the way orthodox Freud-
ians do."[60] Repressing a so-called drive doesn't worry him
because he doesn't think there is such a thing; there are mostly
just cultural norms which parents have a right and duty to enforce—if they can. Dr. Gersh recognizes the pervasiveness of
extra family influences in our culture and he recognizes that
other cultures have done their child rearing differently and
had the children survive.

What he calls "the paranoid style" in American child rearing
assumes, wrongly in his opinion, that parents can be blamed
for everything about their child. Dr. Gersh counters this attitude with a discussion of inherited individual temperamental
differences and the influence of society. It also figures that
a perspective which looks beyond the individual isolated
parent-child relationship, and beyond Freudian emphasis upon
sexuality, also doesn't pontificate about sex roles and the need
to raise "feminine" and "masculine" children. Dr. Gersh
doesn't. Parents are parents, children are children, and essential things like vigilance and babyproofing the house to avoid
accidents are emphasized. The working-mother problem is
omitted. Dr. Gersh rather successfully treads the fine line between encouraging parents to trust themselves and giving them
authoritative warning about the most important problems. He's
authoritarian, but self-consciously so, with a rare irony and
humor. He seems to understand his own assumptions and rec-

[59] Gersh, *op. cit.*
[60] *Ibid.*, p. 109.

ognize and label his theories for the parent reader. You are quite free to disagree, and understand why.

Once again I am brought back to my criteria for judging how-to books by the way they answer the why and what-for questions. Clear presentations of over-all aims and goals and world views clarify specific advice on methods. An authority or expert is less murky and authoritarian the more he explains, and he's also much more likely to be understood, trusted, and followed. If basic connections between goals and methods are shown, it becomes easier for parents to pick and choose what advice they find sensible or what they can apply.

When all is said and done and criticisms and quibbles tendered, I do believe in getting advice from experts. I don't think parents should trust themselves so much that they never try to improve or listen to professionals. Living in a country where there is little attention given in school curricula to child rearing and not much opportunity to go beyond limited personal experience, reading books on one's own is a form of compensatory education. I don't think that a little knowledge is dangerous; nor that too much knowledge makes it harder to rear children. The common American distrust of intellect and thinking should not deter parents from learning all they can about parenting. Nothing dire happens from increased self-consciousness and even a little good guilt over the need to do better is salutory. Only the two extremes should be avoided: presumption and casual carelessness on one hand and paralyzing anxiety and overprotection on the other. And such extremes aren't caused by reading anyway; the how-to books try to steer a middle course and give some idea of what the middle of the road looks like.

I would only emphasize that it is better to read many books rather than one (at least two). If you read different books and see that experts agree and disagree, then it is obvious and easier to choose a course, adding in one's own experience. Effective study in any field helps you learn new information, new theories, new opinions with which you integrate your own experience. The more you attend to a subject, the more you can bring new insight to daily life. One's past personal experience as a child, or present parental experience, interacts with advice and guidance that comes from others, be it in books, on TV, in person. Difficulties will provoke a desire to change and be better but even in a fairly satisfactory situation, one can aspire to do better.

Observers have noted what they rightly call "the rising tide of expectations for happiness and good health that so differentiates this generation of parents from its predecessors."[61] This may lead to frustration at limited abilities to create a good life for one's family, but the urge and desire is a good sign. This desire is behind the writing and reading of how-to parent books, and these books may do an immense amount of good. My criticisms revolve more around the unconscious assumptions the authors make and what they leave out. Their bias and omissions serve to reinforce unfortunate backward-looking aspects in American society. These blind spots can be compensated for by parents who recognize the need to overcome sexist stereotypes, to seek a more social and committed life with more aesthetic experience.

That is the final thing to remember in reading how-to books. After one has seen differences among the different approaches, after one has discerned the theories behind the advice, and the assumptions which guide certain opinions, then one has to decide what has been left out. Parents need to take pains to develop those dimensions and stages of life for their children which have been most nearly ignored in popular guides. Look at it this way, the parents who are creatively rearing their children above and beyond the call of Dr. Spock and colleagues are shaping the how-to books for the next generation. Chil-

[61] *Ibid.*

dren whose parents insist they get more than Ginott says to give will create a new brand of future expert.

The suspicion grows that children's potential has long been unknown, untapped, and undeveloped. The same may very well be said about parents, parent power, and parenting potential. Parents may just be beginning to have their own consciousness raised. They and others begin to ask questions about their rights and role. A new parent-child politics evolves.

Parent-Child Politics

Few discussions of parenthood focus on the relation of parents to all the others involved in parent-child processes. Fewer still take into account the politics of child rearing. Hard questions of power and coercion, rights and duties, privileges and responsibilities are quietly buried in mists of sentiment or psychological snowbanks (sometimes identical). As we see, one marked failure of most how-to parent books is the virtual absence of any treatment of how the outside world impinges upon the family scene.

Parents may generally be isolated in American culture, but they're not that isolated. Parents have to deal with their own parents, siblings, friends, and peers, as well as their children's peers, teachers, and a multitude of authorities, specialists, and experts. Granted, hassles with the police or a child's psychoanalyst may be a relatively rare experience for a parent—with an understanding that the lower classes tend to have more than average parent-police problems and the upper classes more than average parent-psychoanalyst encounters. But even if law and therapy skirmishes are avoided, parents still contact a multitude of others specifically in their roles as parents. Are there any principles governing the politics of parenthood?

I think so. Such principles arise from the primary functions of parenting: to protect, nurture, partner, and prepare an independent adult. These parenting functions are not performed in a vacuum but by individuals operating within a larger group, part of a population. Basically, in my view, the larger population is primarily important and parents mediate the larger group's genetic, linguistic, cultural, and economic structures. Parenting may precede every individual member's advent into the group, but launching an adult into the larger population is the goal of child rearing. Parenting is then only a temporary mandate, a provisional responsibility, an irreversible but one-way commitment that must operate primarily for the advantage of the child's development. In other words, this view places the welfare of the child and the betterment of the whole group before parents, who are but temporary mediators.

Yet we also know that to do a good job for the sake of the child and the group, parents must protect the child from dangers in the environment, and in an imperfect world other members of the group can be as real a danger as any. Therefore, part of a parent's primary function is the protection of his child from other adults and children in the general population who might harm or exploit him. We then get to the interesting situation in which parents must, if need be, protect their child from the group for the group, while the group must, if need be, protect the child from its parents who are but temporarily mandated mediators of the group. Both the parents and the rest of the community serve a real function for each child, with corresponding rights and responsibilities. No wonder it's a confusing problem in law, ethics, and everyday life.

If a social group does not give parents enough authority or power, then parents may be helpless and forced to abdicate their protective function. Children can then be subjected to a totalitarian state's upbringing (Russia, China) or their well-being subjected to an institution's power. Without parental rights, power, and aggression, children can be maltreated in orphanages, schools, hospitals, or in jobs, employment, and the armed services. Almost any harassed authority, expert, or specialist in our complicated American scene can be guilty of ignoring or maltreating an improperly protected child. We don't have children pulling coal cars in the mines any more and we don't countenance using children for experimental research (yet), but in between there's still a wide area where parental protection is necessary. Protective parent power is good for the individual child and, therefore, good for the general population which the well-reared adolescent enters.

Parental rights, although temporary, also provide a counter-sphere of influence to the group as a whole. As we remember in *Brave New World*, the rebel against the system started out with a deviant mother, who actually bore a child in her womb instead of going the prescribed test-tube-baby route. This regressive deviance on her part prepared her son to question the established verities. Throughout history we find actual examples of great men and women whose parents raised them (perhaps inadvertently) to question the accepted norms of the group.

As Robert Coles has said so well in a discussion of personal psycho-history:

"And as to those mothers and fathers whom we have all learned to approach with such foreboding, perhaps their influence is indeed decisive. Perhaps Leonardo, Conrad, Abraham Lincoln or Gandhi, Zapata or César Chavez, Mao or De Gaulle slowly learned much from their parents: determination and patience; a capacity for deep attachments or passionate involvements; glimpses into all sorts of things; suspicions about how corrupt a given society is; a store of knowledge; a host of skills or talents; an appreciation of the world's complexity; encouragement to stretch the imagination; an aptness for words; a sharpness of vision; a readiness to listen or speak in such a way that others listen; a turn of mind that is a bit different; a taste for the nuances of meaning or emotion."[1] Obviously, too extreme a deviance may produce madness and crime, but to eliminate parental diversity will eliminate an important source of human creativity. If the processes of natural selection thrives on the variety provided by sexual reproduction and outbreeding, so group culture can be said to benefit from the variety and diversity found in individual unique parenting.

On the other hand, there is a minimum and a limit to the freedom or deviation that the group can grant to individual parents. In asserting the larger group's protective mandate, the group can only permit private parental power to go so far. How far is too far? That is the question. And the answer may differ in different areas of life at different times; religious questions, educational questions, health questions may be settled in different ways. Conflicts over acceptable basic minimums can change as the culture changes. By the time a question gets to the courts in our society there has been a very serious breach of cultural consensus. At that point parent-child politics becomes a legal issue which touches the deepest value questions in our tradition. The very fact that the values of parenting are so embedded in our cultural tradition keeps these parent-child legal questions from being fully developed and clear. These issues have for so long been governed by consensus and cultural assumptions that they resist both definition and change. Before venturing farther into these deep waters, there are other more immediate and concrete areas of parent-child politics which need to be examined.

While a parent is living with his temporary mandate and carrying out his responsibility, what is the role of all the others?

[1] Robert Coles, "Shrinking History—Part One," *The New York Review of Books*, Vol. XX, No. 2 (February 22, 1973), p. 20.

What part is played by people outside the parent-child interaction? We shall ignore for the moment the psychological influences of others through their part in prior conditioning, education, and modeling of parents and just concentrate on the outsiders' direct function. In what immediate ways do others exercise power and influence? First of all the larger group functions as a witness and so exercises some protective supervision of parenting. Along with witness and informal supervision some concrete support and help should be forthcoming. Equally important, those surrounding and interacting with parent and child will provide corrective information to parents. How a child interacts with others, with relatives, with peers, in school and other institutions—these contacts help communicate to parents how their child is functioning.

Since parents get so involved with their children they often find it hard to see them whole. Outsiders can offer distance, new perspectives, new information, different evaluations of both the child and the parenting he's getting. Often, parents can see a reflection of themselves and what they are doing when they and the child meet outsiders—a condition which increases as a child begins his life beyond the parental sphere. A world outside the family and home is absolutely necessary to supplement parent-child interaction. No parents can rear children well without a community. Parents need the support and reflective response of their cloud of witnesses just as a child needs his peers and other adults in order to learn about the world and himself. Both parent and child need the reinforcement, confirmation, and corrective checks of outsiders.

But from a parent's point of view, priorities are clear: Their overwhelming commitment should be to their child. My country right or wrong may be a poor approach to citizenship, but my child right or wrong is an appropriate approach to parenting. The point of parenthood is to provide the beginning of each human life with an absolutely prejudiced protector who will take his side against the world. Come hell or high water, no matter what, the parent is committed to his child. If parents don't take their powerless child's side, who will? It's the first and foremost parental mandate: Be your child's advocate in the world.

Protection, unfortunately, has to begin at home in the family. I am convinced that two parents are more adaptive than one; not only because they can better protect and provide for the child in the outside world, but because they can protect the child from each other. When one parent is distraught or enraged or particularly beaten down or offended with a child, the other parent may keep a positive perspective. It's not so much that a father protects the child from smothering mother love or that the mother protects the child from father's jealous anger and demands; but simply that two people-parents are less likely to lose control simultaneously. With mutual support, consultation, correction, and spelling off of caretaking, fewer breakdowns of parenting are likely. In our pressure-cooker society, there's a bit of the child-abuser in every parent, which supportive parent partners help suppress.

Mated parents also help protect their child against the parents' own parents and family. Having a child together makes for new blood relations to counter the kinship claims of one's family of origin. It's important that a new parent put his child's welfare before the claims of his own parents and assorted relatives. If a new parent is still dominated by his or her parents or run by the ideas and criticism of relatives, the child will not be properly protected. Future-oriented American culture cannot operate with too much filial submission, or non-parental interference. The extended family cannot sufficiently protect any individual, so a growing child has to be protected from an extended family's demands. Caught up in a system demanding individualistic independence, parents must choose their child's future growth over the claims of the past embodied in their parents and kin.

Parents cannot offer their children as sacrificial gifts to their own parents. Nor can they allow a child to become a scapegoat or be caught up in an ongoing generational struggle.[2] Despite any family disapproval or conflict, parents have to be committed to their own unique child, following the dictates of their own judgment and conscience. Standing up to one's family to make independent parental decisions is a final rite of adulthood. It's also the best chance a child has for getting proper parental commitment and protection. Change comes into child rearing and the culture because Americans are willing to break with their own parents and seek a better way for their children. Our children shall not be beaten with belts. They shall go on to school. They will not go into the mines, or factory. They will go to the doctor or psychotherapist, no matter what Grandma thinks.

Intergenerational conflict is almost unavoidable in our mobile changing culture—so, to some extent, is conflict with other relatives. Since each family member can choose from a pluralistic array of lifestyles and central values, kinfolk will often be at odds. In America the closest of kin have the delicate task of communicating to each other values, opinions, and even criticism while choosing a course of action independent of the extended family. Family interference in child rearing is only countenanced in severe breakdowns of the nuclear family. Discontinuity is so great in many families that parents dread premature death, partly at the thought of their children being raised by their own parents or siblings. Even where there's love and affection, there may also be deep disagreements. In a way, parents get their first experience as protectors, fending off their own kin. Naturally this also goes for spoiling and too much

[2] R. D. Laing, *The Politics of the Family and Other Essays* (New York: Vintage Books, 1969).

positive interference. It may be almost impossible to spoil a baby or get too much adult attention directed toward a child, but when overstimulation and overprivilege is the problem, then parents have to have the courage to set and stick to limits, no matter whose feelings are hurt.

Whether in the family or out, another problem exists. The urge toward competitive parenting is almost demonic today— throughout all classes. Parents constantly interacting with their friends, peers, and fellow parents can be sorely tempted to push their children for their own status. Competition is a fact of life, of course, and every parent wants to be proud of a child; but there is a more insidious stage in which the welfare of the child becomes less important to the parent than the approval the child can bring to him as a parent. Very subtly, the observers of the family, with their outsider's opinions, become more important to the parents than the actual child. Other-directed parents concentrating on their own reputation are murderous because they do not shrink from drastic means to get children to measure up.[3]

Small allegories of the basic problem are played out in many a public place, especially grocery stores, for some reason. Parents are ashamed if a child transgresses some rule of deportment and in face-saving anger literally assault the child. In public places all over America, children are hit, pushed, shaken, and pinched by their parents while subjected to streams of invective and verbal abuse. The hostility of the parent against the child arises because the parent abandons his role as the child's protector in the world and identifies instead with the hostile observers who judge, criticize, and resent children's "bad" behavior. In these incidents the parent fails to be the child's parent-advocate and becomes one with anti-child America. Occasionally a parent whose child is upset in front of others has enough secure confidence to maintain unapologetic poise

[3] R. D. Laing and A. Esterson, *Sanity, Madness and the Family* (Baltimore: Penguin Books, 1970).

and expect outsiders to understand and offer help. The attitude is child-centered: How can all of us as mature nurturing adults help this troubled child with his difficulty? Such protective parental behavior places a demand on outsiders to have empathy with a child. Often the tactic works to activate latent nurturing attitudes, usually submerged in quick criticism.

When older children "get into trouble" or offend outsiders in some way, the same choice is open to parents. They can turn on their child for having subjected them to embarrassment, as well as for the breach of conduct, or they can remain their child's advocate. The best parent resists being shifted into a hostile outsider's point of view, more ready to judge, accuse, shame, and punish a child than anyone else. Questions of status and reputation are secondary to the child's welfare. The more secure parent stays on his child's side and tries to assess the conflict from the child's point of view.

This does not mean that one's child will always be judged innocent and guiltless, far from it. That's the other perversion of parental protection, to always deny any flaw or fault in one's child. Assuming automatic guilt or automatic innocence are perennial parental defenses which do not help children. Parents should be able to give their own child at least as much support as a lawyer who is still going to be on the side of his client no matter what the facts are or who's to blame. But unlike a lawyer, a parent also knows that one very important part of his role is to help his child adapt to the world and survive. This may sometimes mean letting a child take some lumps which would be undeserved in a pure system of justice, but which are par for the course in this world. A parent who is too aggressive on the behalf of a child and strives to make an issue of every injustice can spend his whole life doing nothing else —children are subject to too many indignities.[4]

4 Norman K. Denzin, "Wednesday's Child—Introduction to special issue, Crusade Against Children," *Trans-Action*, Vol. 8 (July–August 1971), pp. 28–29.

Parent-child politics is also, like real politics, the art of the possible. If you're thoroughly enmeshed in an unjust system, you can't expect one parent to revolutionize everything. Few parents are willing to sacrifice their children to a cause. Great efforts for reform are best done in organized groups and at propitious moments when there is a chance of success. (The civil rights struggle for integrated schools, for instance.) On a day-to-day basis a parent may often have to compromise, and teach compromise to children.

It's not fair, but life is not fair, and the child has to learn to adapt to a certain amount of injustice to survive. No ghetto parent or long-haired teen-ager's parent, for instance, could ever advise resisting police injustice on the street; the child could be killed or injured seriously beyond the help of parents or a lawyer. Seeking their child's welfare, parents as advocates have to judge each case of conflict and decide when and how to intervene. But at least they can be honest with their children and tell a child that his perception of injustice and flaws in the system (school, police, army) is correct. Better to inculcate some healthy cynicism and alienation from the Establishment than to make a child distrust his own perception of reality. For parents blindly to defend all operations of the powers that be is to encourage maladaptive blindness. The best parental compromise is to only partially legitimate the system.

On the other hand, a parent can use power and influence to demand of his child more than adaptation to the local political realities. A child may be avoiding all conflict and getting along swimmingly with others outside. Yet the parents know that this success is a bad sign. Often in parent-child politics, peace at any price is a destructive principle. Parents should sometimes worry over their child fitting in too well; they can act to stir up discontent, to set up other standards of judgment. If parents do not provide a counterinfluence to the going system, the snug fit may be smothering. Some discontinuity in worlds seems absolutely necessary for growth. Or maybe here, too, survival can be at stake. In times when worlds crash regularly, the totally adapted person who was a popular cipher in some system goes down. It's the fatal flaw of aristocracies and upper classes who overprotect their children from all the raw rubbing of not fitting in. Parents who are obsessed with conformity, respectability, and fitting in to popular ideals are not protecting their children from a most subtle danger. Parents can sometimes protect by encouraging deviance and engendering conflict.

The necessity of conflict becomes very apparent in the relationship of a parent to his child's peers. A child absolutely needs a peer group to grow with—without peers he can never separate from parents, never test himself in many crucial ways, and never learn things he will need to know in order to function as an adult. No adult can give a child what playmates and peers can give. Adults, be they parents or friends, cannot help but be larger, smarter, and irreversibly distant from childhood. They can make efforts to modify their powers and play at a child's level, but it is not the same. Inequality is always there. So is the civilization factor. No adult could deliver to a child the naïve blows and accolades of one's peers. Few normal adults can stand the juvenilia of juveniles, or take the time for extended meanderings on the outskirts of their own social system.

Not only are peer relationships of the young found in every culture, but they are found in primate social systems as well. It seems a necessary intermediate term between infancy and adulthood in any social group. The juvenile stage is different according to the particular social structure of the adult group it is preparing for, but it always includes some playful practice of adult roles.[5] Thus young male monkeys engage in playful

[5] Sherwood L. Washburn, "Aggressive Behavior and Human Evolution," *Social Change and Human Behavior*, George V. Coelho and Eli A. Rubinstein, eds. (Maryland: National Institute of Mental Health, 1972), pp. 21–39.

fighting and rough-and-tumble play which prepares them for mating processes. Young females attend more to infants and stay more closely with the females in a troop.[6] Here the relationship with peers is also a means of separating from the mother. It is quite clear, however, that parenting in primates determines to a great extent the fate of the offspring in the juvenile peer group.

Dominance in some primate hierarchies seems to be catching. A dominant mother seems to be able to pass on her status to her offspring.[7] This may happen through paternal procuring of more food or more protection or more time and energy for grooming and maternal care. Whatever gives young monkeys a head start, it shows up with their peers. But they are still on their own eventually. Harlow tells charming stories of his monkey mothers who are torn by conflict when they have to let their offspring venture out into the peer group.[8] There is a lot of pulling offspring back to mother and indecision on the mother's part. When the child gets beyond her reach (these are caged monkeys) the mother watches how her youngster is making out in the rough-and-tumble play; she even tries to intervene if her offspring is getting the worst of it. Apparently some hostility builds up between mothers and the members of her offspring's peer group. Teasing of mothers by the juvenile band is observed.

These observations of monkeys provoke irresistible (if rash) analogies to bands of human juveniles. What neighborhood

[6] Harry F. Harlow, "The Heterosexual Affectional System in Monkeys," *Interpersonal Dynamics*, Warren G. Bennis, Edgar H. Schein, Fred I. Steele and David E. Berlew, eds. (Homewood, Illinois: The Dorsey Press, 1968), pp. 43–60.

[7] Charles Kaufman, "Biologic Considerations of Parenthood," *Parenthood: Its Psychology and Psychopathology*, E. James Anthony and Therese Benedek, eds. (Boston: Little, Brown & Co., 1970), p. 9.

[8] Harry F. Harlow, "The Maternal Affectional System," *Determinants of Infant Behavior II*, ed., B. M. Foss (New York: John Wiley & Sons, 1963), pp. 3–33.

has ever lacked the mother who fought and yelled at the neighborhood gang on behalf of her darling child. The wariness of all youth toward all parents is in these cases a mutual persecution. The child always suffers because of the mother's overzealous defense tactics, but often these children can never resist calling on parents for defense. When parents overprotect, they inflame latent intergenerational hostility. Parents can ruin their child's relationships with his peers, setting the child too apart and disturbing the usual growth that comes from being an uneasy member of a gang.

At the other extreme is the underprotecting parent who abandons his child to his peers either through neglect or some distorted idea of independence. Like the monkey at the bottom of the dominance hierarchy, the child without protectors has a hard time with his age-mates. With no home territory behind him, back to the sea, he has to be dependent on the group. Sensing weakness and dependency the group exacts service. As we see in *The Lord of the Flies* and in real-life urban gangs, the absence of parental influence can produce barbarism. Urie Bronfenbrenner, the noted child expert, even grades the Western countries of the world on the extent that parent-absent-peer culture has induced social disarray.[9] He maintains that when peer influence becomes more dominant than adult and parental socialization, then a society is in trouble.

From the point of view of parent-child politics, it's obvious that two centers of power and influence have to be in some tension for optimal growth. Parents have to exert a strong influence which counters the pressure of the peer group. Parents and parental figures inculcate values, standards, aspirations, and ideals of the adult world. The peer group usually rebels and exerts a present-oriented pull to the here and now. Parents may be conservative where the youth group is daring,

9 Urie Bronfenbrenner, *Two Worlds of Childhood: U.S. and U.S.S.R.* (New York: Russell Sage Foundation, 1970), 115–19.

and parents may push and dare where peers stress conservative conformity to the going norm. A growing child can play each system's pull against each other to find his own growing room and his own place in the world. Each allegiance keeps the other from being an emotional tyranny. Each can be a retreat from the demands of the other, preparing a growing child to re-enter each arena at increasingly advanced levels.

Parents should understand this dynamic and not shrink from their role as "enemies of freedom," the "squarest of the square," "persecutor" of friends. Parents have to lose the power struggle, it's disastrous to win; but it should be a long-drawn-out process in which the growing child wins no more freedom than he is really able to cope with. Ideally, by the time he has overcome his parent's authority in order to join his peers, he is strong enough and smart enough to withstand peer pressure. Parental charisma and clout should last until a healthy cynicism over peer pressure begins. Since parents can rarely control the peer group, the best they can do is to make sure their children are not subservient to it psychologically. If they can help their children to be more independent and confident, they may even insure a child's leadership of his group.

There are also a few strategies open to parents when peer pressure seems to be a negative influence. Parents can try to provide alternate groups of peers. Fight peers with peers. The poor send their children to visit relatives or to take jobs in new locations. The rich use camps, travel, summer vacations, private schools, and jobs and relatives to provide alternate peer groups of young people. Even when things are going well, parents do well to loosen the grip of youthful social circles by broadening the world view of their parochial children. Many young people tend to be xenophobic and sink into the comforting conformity of a customary circle. Children need both stability and a sense of belonging, along with alternatives and opportunities for new beginnings. After all, prophets get no honor in their own country because their peers pigeonhole them into a place and a role which is as stifling as it is cozy. A child can get so bound by a set reputation and role that it's hard to break out to grow. Parents have to fight negative reputations which tend to be self-fulfilling. Going into a far country for a while allows for a new beginning on one's return.

Parents try to manipulate the social environment so that their children will have positive experiences with their peers, several different sets of peers. They can make their home a gathering place where children are welcome when the home is set up for hospitality. This can help in parental supervision and help to shape a peer group's standards. A friendly parent who is willing to exercise firm parenting while welcoming children is enough of a novelty to be attractive. When development is going smoothly there may be many positive almost familial relationships between parents and their children's peers. If there is conflict or deep disagreement, however, latent parent-peer hostility may come to the fore. Usually a certain distance is inevitable, since the friend has to remain the child's and cannot be co-opted into intimacy and direct involvement with a parent. A child's friends have to be his own.[10]

Eventually parental influence and peer influence make way for the coupling of courtship and marriage. Parents and friends are left behind in order to start a peer-pair bond of intimacy and commitment.[11] Parents lose first, and then peers lose for the sake of new matings. The cycle begins anew. Parents have a whole new set of negotiations and enlarged family politics to manage—in-laws, grandchildren, and other relatives by marriage. Hopefully, by the time children reach marriage, the parents' protective role has been outgrown. Power in our social

10 Harry Stack Sullivan, *Conceptions of Modern Psychiatry* (New York: W. W. Norton, 1953), Chapter 15, "The Juvenile Era," pp. 227–44.
11 Erik H. Erikson, *Childhood and Society*, 2d. ed. (New York: W. W. Norton, 1963), pp. 263–66.

system is usually equalized between parents and their grown children. The ultimate aim of parent-child politics resembles the divesting of Empire and colonies in order to get full-fledged partners. The alliance of equals may continue in a commonwealth, but the independence of all members helps the whole.

But as all historians know, it can be a rocky road to political independence. Parents who are involved in the bloodless revolution have to become expert politicians along the way. Not only must they protect children from kin, friends, and negotiate as best they can with peers, but they have to deal with beneficent institutions. The foremost of these is, of course, school. While camps, recreation, and cultural programs and so on are also child-filled institutions, school is now mandatory.[12] Parents need a little red book to aid them in the guerrilla campaigns they may have to wage with various schools. The ideal maintains that parent and school co-operate as partners—but then even Chiang and Mao were once in a common front. Family experience with school, from nursery to college, can vary all the way in a spectrum from execrable to ecstatic. Most public schools in middle-class areas are classically mediocre, somewhere in the middle.

At the moment, debates in the society are raging over the effectiveness of schools. Talk of "deschooling"[13] society alternates with studies which show that family status and not the school determines the successes or inequalities of society.[14] Supposedly, how the child comes into school is more important than anything learned while there. Who can tell how this public debate on education will turn out? But in the meantime children have to go to school and parents need to know how

[12] Peter F. Drucker, "School Around the Bend," *Psychology Today*, Vol. 6 (June 1972), pp. 49–54; and Theodore R. Sizer, *Places for Learning Places for Joy* (Cambridge, Massachusetts: Harvard University Press, 1973).

[13] Ivan Illich, *De-Schooling Society* (New York: Harper & Row, 1972).

[14] Godfrey Hodgson, "Do Schools Make A Difference?" *The Atlantic*, (March 1973), pp. 35–46.

to cope, especially with ordinary day-to-day parent-school interaction.

Only in special situations can parents band together and create enough political power to radically change a school system.[15] But almost anywhere the school board and school officials are responsive to organized parent-power, if you have knowledgeable, determined leaders and a cause capable of inspiring and unifying all parents to get major changes. Most parents, however, are not up to these major efforts; they can only operate at much lower levels of activity, without much group cohesiveness. Ordinarily it's usually a one-on-one operation, parent-to-teacher or parent-to-school official. These interactions are always governed by the fact that while the child is a hostage in the power of the school system, the school needs the support and approval of parents in order to keep running.

In fact, the more power and status the parents have the better the school will be. Money will be spent on facilities, supplies, and good teachers. This situation follows the old law that the more children have, the more they get, while the deprived and needy get less and less. In school matters, only the very, very rich can demand that the school actually serve the child. Only the rich can provide alternate education and apply the pressure of their gifts and tuitions to shape the school as an institution. Alternate schools and free schools among the poor are always open to social and financial pressure along with harassment. They are rare and have trouble surviving. Middle-class, middle-range public schools survive and are pressured to be minimally good, but they still don't put children's education first.[16]

[15] Ellen Lurie, *How to Change the Schools* (New York: Vintage Books, 1970).

[16] Norman K. Denzin, "Children and Their Caretakers," *Trans-Action* (July–August 1971), pp. 62–72; John Holt, *How Children Fail* (New York: Pitman, 1964); Jonathan Kozol, *Death at an Early Age* (Boston: Houghton Mifflin, 1967).

Schools like any other institution become a vested interest filled with people who are intent on keeping their own position within the system. Education is now a big business, employing many people, purchasing supplies, building buildings. When education of children successfully competes with the business aspects of the system, there remains the real problem of deciding whose interest the school serves. Public schools often see themselves as the agent of the state, or of the local community of taxpayers, or more covertly, of the educational establishment. In any of these perspectives it's not the child's place to reason why, theirs but to do or die, etc. Parents are expected to be the back-up field commanders, sending their children off, even if into the valley of death, at an early age. At least they are off the streets and out of the labor pool, in one version of the *real* society-school contract. A skeptical parent has a real dilemma.

If a parent is too critical, cynical, and combative against the works and pomps of school, it will affect his child's attitude. Children who tend to be lazy and rebellious will take their cue from the parents' attitude in order to balk, rebel, and raise hell. Parents can help destroy the legitimacy of school authority. Taking a totally negative attitude children can miss whatever is good in school while stunting their own academic progress. Since each child has to spend a long, long time in school, the best tactic of survival is not stubborn and sullen withdrawal. As every inhabitant of a prison camp or prison knows, the best survival tactic is to be actively superorganized, work the system to the hilt, and self-improve like crazy. All inmates, soldiers, patients, and students can do a lot to control their leaders and keepers by selective re-enforcement. You perform for the good guys seeking reforms, bolster their morale and power in the system so their numbers can increase.

Parents have to encourage their children in the same positively aggressive attitudes. So it's an imperfect system in which we're all stuck; how can we make the best of it? Surely the best way to bring out the best in any teacher is to co-operate, support, and stimulate, without threatening. Teachers also get discouraged by criticism, apathy, hostility, and generally bad vibrations. The more support a teacher gets for creativity, the more he or she will dare move in that direction. And the same goes for school administrators. Parents in a middling school system ought to try and overcome inadequacies with positive support, at least up to tolerable limits. The growing movement to have parents volunteer in the schools is a step in the right direction. The presence of parents in the schools is almost always a positive improvement. Adults around help keep petty tyrannies under control (passes, verbal harassment, etc.), and they help break down the age segregation which leads to a sense of social unreality with consequent disorders.

In other words, in day-to-day parent-school politics the best strategy is intrusive support. Go to school as much as you can. Go to meetings, conferences, performances, visiting days, and any other times you can talk to teachers and administrators. Volunteer and get as involved as possible; fight for money, programs, and buildings. Parents who get educated about education, and involved, help break the grip of the education establishment and broaden the base of the school's support. The schools can only be humanized by infiltration and intervention. The more parental response and parent power, the more alert the administration. I'd like to see parental evaluation of teachers go into the files for tenure decisions, along with student response. Since individual parents differ so much in lifestyle and philosophy, there might well be some mechanism for sorting and choosing different classroom styles and learning approaches for different families. Experimental schools within schools can sometimes do this.

When a parent does see an individual teacher in teacher conferences, very basic attitudes need to be conveyed. A parent needs to show a respect for the teacher's job and even more important a deep respect for one's child. The contractual model is a good one to follow. The teacher's part in the contract is to teach by encouraging the child's learning and self-respect; and the parent's role is to encourage the child and co-operatively supplement in all possible ways. Teachers have to tell the parent what they are trying to do, and parents have to tell teachers what they expect, what they would like, and how they see the situation. In their parental role as protectors, parents have to communicate their demand that the teacher fulfill his proper role. What are you doing for my child? How are you helping his development? What can I do to help you do a good job?

Enough aggressive respect and interest have to be shown so that the teacher knows this child is not without supporters and protection. The teacher is not a critic judging the child and making one-way demands. The child and the parent have rightful claims to professional competence and service. Through a serious respect for the profession, parents can press their demands and expectations on the teacher. Teachers in their professional roles can make demands upon the child and parents. The teacher can also offer a professional evaluation of the child's development. If a parent feels that the teacher has overstepped his rightful authority or been counterproductive in his methods (shaming the child or verbal abuse), the parent should vigorously complain and point this out.[17] The privacy of the classroom covers a multitude of abuses as well as heroic efforts beyond the call of duty.

On the issue of school punishment, I think parents should take a firm and active stand. No adult teacher hits my child, throws things at him, pinches, pulls his hair, or throws him around (all examples from personal experience in an enlight-

[17] Dr. Thomas Gordon, *Parent Effectiveness Training* (New York: Peter H. Wyden, 1971), pp. 298–306.

ened suburban school system). Whatever the law in the state, parents should fight physical punishment in school. Abuses of power are too frequent to allow corporal punishment, especially in a system in which adults have power over children without witnesses or controls. I think parents ought to make an issue of verbal abuse, too. No adult would publicly abuse another adult verbally for fear of libel. Children who above all things need self-respect and a good self-image should never be subject to abusive treatment by an adult. We don't allow flogging in the army, or let employers physically punish employees; barbarism is barbarism. The schools already hold more than enough power, with their authority to grade, create evaluative files, suspend and give credentials needed in employment.

More and more frequently parents have to protect their children by asserting their children's civil rights in institutions supposedly dedicated to their welfare, but tempted to abuses of power. A basic parental stance of demanding respect and giving respect is probably the best protective strategy. It's also important to intrude, volunteer, and serve in order to supervise and strengthen necessary institutions. The more voluntary the institution, such as camp, religious school, artistic and recreational programs, the more parents can exert parent protection.[18] Withdrawal is optional. But in schools, hospitals, disciplinary institutions, or the army, parents are caught in the bind of necessary submission to authority. It takes more guile, endurance, and active effort to protect a child. When it's a case of law and coercion, parents may have to know about existing laws and lobby for the civil rights of their children.

In times past, and perhaps still in many parts of the country, parents have never had to cope with such complex difficulties or confrontations. The homogenous community runs along smoothly on cultural consensus and the co-operation of all

[18] Mary Perkins Ryan, *We're All in This Together* (New York: Holt, Rinehart & Winston, 1972).

concerned. Legal questions and civil rights for children are distant, almost irrelevant, areas of parental concern. All the local institutions, authorities, and official posts are filled with friends, neighbors, and relatives. Parents do not have to aggressively protect their children because the whole community is organized for mutual protection and support. Parents hardly come into contact with any strangers and have few dealings with outside experts and specialists. Communication and mutual interaction are far easier when all parties share a common background. Even the power differential which sets up the expert professional versus layman can be muted in a stable homogenous community in which there is familiarity and mutual dependence.

But for most American parents today, professional experts, authorities, and specialists can present problems. The basic situation is one in which the parent confronts a professional who has something that the parent needs for his child. Be it doctor, lawyer, priest, teacher, policeman, social worker, psychotherapist, or some other expert professional, the parent has a challenge. The parent must succeed in communicating his own view of the child's needs to the expert as well as elicit and understand the expert's response or decision. Once the parent understands the professional's viewpoint, goal, and methods, the parent has to pass judgment and decide on his own co-operation or resistance. Parental co-operation or resistance comes in various levels and degrees, some of which is consciously controlled. Communication, mutual understanding, and basic trust become crucial ingredients in these encounters. The parent first has to comprehend and then decide how much to trust the expert's opinions and directions. Failures in communication and lack of empathy and trust keep parents from being able to take advantage of the professional's expertise and vice versa.

A classic case of difficulties in communication has been observed in doctor-patient exchanges in a pediatrics emergency room.[19] The conversations between parents and doctors were recorded, and follow-up studies done to see whether the parents followed the doctor's advice. Unfortunately, physicians who are trained in medicine were not found to be very skilled in communication; they used technical language in a confusing way and made little effort to deal with the personal aspects of the situation—one in which parents were anxious and upset over their children. The physicians did not make effective contact as often as they should have; and parents (mostly mothers) did not follow the doctors' directions through lack of understanding and lack of trust in them as persons. If the doctor did not convey real interest in the total welfare of the family, then the parents did not feel very obliged to follow his directions.

I think these same difficulties occur often in parent-professional encounters. The expert professional defines his role ideally as a helper, but when personal interest dries up into professional cool, then the expert loses his client's allegiance and co-operation. Some professionals can be very condescending, if not callous. They can intimidate parents; and sometimes this is done on purpose, in order to get compliance and respect. But what's usually provoked in such situations is but a superficial acquiescence followed by resistance. Unless the professional expert can convey the conviction that he is a concerned partner with the parent, an ally in working toward the child or family's welfare, then the expertise is useless.

An aggressive enough parent can usually activate a truly contractual partnership in most professionals. Parents can get results if they have enough self-confidence to demand that the professional communicate *clearly* in understandable language and relate his expertise to the whole picture. Asking pressing

[19] Barbara M. Korsch and Vida Francis Negrete, "Doctor-Patient Communication," *Scientific American*, Vol. 227 (August 1972), pp. 66–74.

questions and demanding clear answers take a lot of nerve and verbal facility. The silencing strategies of professional experts are legion. If there were a Saul Alinsky to organize parents in the pursuit of their rights and interests, he could concentrate on communicating skills, or techniques for pushing professionals to the wall. What do you mean exactly? What do you propose to do, exactly? Why should I do what you advise and how do I do it? Clearly, understanding and personal assent motivate the most parental co-operation.

The crisis of credibility and legitimacy in our society has reached such proportions that many parents share in a general distrust of authority. There may be people left who slavishly follow some professional authority (probably their psychoanalyst, astrologer, or internist), but, generally, priest, policeman, lawyer, educator, and social worker are often suspected of feathering their own nest and looking out for their own welfare. Parents have to judge each case, each confrontation, trying to be wise as a serpent and innocent as a dove on behalf of their children. If I am too suspicious and resistant, I may be harming my child who will be helped if I follow this expert's advice. On the other hand, I as a parent may know my child better than anyone and have access to the inside story over a long time span. Perhaps this expert's opinion does not apply to my child's case. Many a child has been harmed by mislabeling, misdiagnoses, or the too pessimistic or optimistic prognosis of some specialist.

As usual, the parents' recourse lies in checks and balances, to get more professional and lay opinions as the situation escalates in seriousness. After consulting different sources of expertise, a better judgment can be made on the relative worth of each, or the range of opinions within which the decisions have to be made. The only danger in this course is that parents may deny and resist bad news to such an extent that they will never settle down and get help for the child. The cultural pressure to be the perfect parent with the perfect child in a family with no problems has to be resisted. Many a parent, for instance, faced with the drug epidemic and their child's drug use, denies everything and utterly fails to get help for his child. Parental panic sometimes creates paralysis.

The agony and suffering that parents go through with their children's problems, as in cases of drug abuse, tend to produce every kind of denial, defense, and resistance. Parents are so vulnerable that they can be sorely tempted to wishful distortions of reality. Parental self-deceit must be the most potent brand of all; Mrs. Oswald still considers her son a good boy, a hero. In so many cases parents are blind to all warnings, all advice, all response from experts and professionals who have contact with a child. The two destructive extremes of parental response are everywhere apparent; there are the parents who deny and resist all professional help and advice and there are the parents who abandon their children to any and all professional experts—especially those who will remove a troublesome child from the scene. In the latter cases children are put into homes as incorrigible, sent to reform schools, handed over to the police and the courts, put in mental hospitals and sent to dreadful schools and camps without a qualm or due process.[20] When parental protection breaks down, it can result in benighted resistance to any and all professional help or abandonment to professional expertise.

So far we have been speaking of ways in which parents have to protect their children from members of the larger population. But the other side of the question is raised with a recognition of parental failure. The larger population, professionals, and lay members of the community have to protect the child from parental abuses of power. Such perversions of parenting have to be faced as an unpleasant reality. There is a strong

[20] Paul Lerman, "Child Convicts," *Trans-Action*, (July–August 1971), pp. 35–44.

tendency to deny the fact that parents can be harmful to health and well-being.[21] But there are active abuses and negative abuses in parenting. Negatively, parents abuse by denying the needs of their children and not providing the necessities; they simply abandon the children and withdraw all parental support, protection, and supervision. Active parental abuses of power entail physical or psychological persecutions, punishments, and attacks.[22] Naturally the two forms of parental breakdown are closely related and present equally delicate problems to the community at large.[23]

How, after all, do you protect a child from its parents when in general, under normal conditions, a child's greatest protection is parental authority, autonomy, and responsibility? The power and rights that the group gives to a parent for the sake of protecting and rearing a child can be abused and used against the child. Socially and legally you must construct some way to support the rights and functions of parents who do well while supplanting or restraining the parents who are harming their children. Since there are few substitutes for parental care, financially, emotionally, or socially, parent-child bonds cannot be broken lightly. It is far better to construct ways in which help can be provided to prevent parental breakdown, abandonment, and abuse. But who is to judge and set the standards on behalf of the children? The whole movement to define such difficult questions and decide on legislation has evolved as a Children's Rights movement.

I think this is the only way to approach the problem. Instead of seeing the child as a form of private property with the non-citizen status of a slave or animal, it should be recognized

[21] Sanford N. Katz, *When Parents Fail: The Law's Response to Family Breakdown* (Boston: Beacon Press, 1971).

[22] David G. Gil, *Violence Against Children: Physical Child Abuse in the United States* (Cambridge: Harvard University Press, 1970).

[23] Serapio R. Zalba, "Battered Children," *Trans-Action* (July–August, 1971), pp. 58–60.

that the child is specially valued. True, in an earlier American philosophy of parent-child relationships, the child and his parents belonged to God, and the parent (particularly the father) was God's servant on earth, given a divine right of authority over his family. There really did exist a seventeenth-century Massachusetts law by which a man could put a stubborn or rebellious son over sixteen to death. (But could you catch such a son with a wilderness to hide in?)[24] Then too, the authority of the religious establishment was strong, constraining by its force the family's authority over children, or at least ensuring ideals, limits, and social supervision by the congregation. Today, religious authority has lost the constraining power of social consensus. In the vacuum, children have been increasingly considered in a much older view as belonging to the parents as a form of private property, or to the state as future citizens.

Neither philosophy of ownership seems acceptable, in the American value system. No government can own its members, but instead should serve the people with a care not to oppress and invade the rights of citizens. Surely, parents cannot own their children, because since the Civil War we have determined that no human being can be owned by another. Perhaps a valid parent-child politics can assert that each human being belongs to the whole human species, past, present, and future. This approach gives tradition its due (or the dead their equal votes) but, by an emphasis upon the future, keeps enough uncertainty in the equation to curtail any present community from exercising total control. Practically, this means that the present system of law decides how to administer the trust of the species so neither parents nor government can impinge on the rights of children. In other words, the rather vague but slowly expanding legal doctrine of *parens patriae* has to be defined and developed. This claimed power of the state to intervene

[24] Oscar Handlin and Mary F. Handlin, *Facing Life: Youth and the Family in American History* (Boston: Little, Brown & Co., 1971).

as ultimate protector in parental rights, according to one authority, "is said to have originated in England in the seventeenth century. It is generally explained as being derived from the Sovereign's prerogative in protecting his subjects unable to protect themselves, that is, mental incompetents and infants."[25] Slowly but surely the state has become more directly and actively involved in the parent-child relationship, but in a piecemeal confusing way.

There seem to be many difficulties to be overcome in clarifying the vague situation. There needs to be some consensus on what basic minimums of parental care should be. Current definitions hardly take enough account of psychological welfare or emotional needs of children beyond the necessities. But then only in the last twenty years has the problem of active physical child abuse by parents come to public attention or been subject to any legislative controls.[26] Growing out of a new awareness of very serious and growing problems in parenting, perhaps a more widespread and complex consensus of acceptable parental behavior could be determined. Since child abuse has been defined in response to recent findings, I think new agreements could be reached on minimum parental responsibilities incorporating many of the ongoing decisions and definitions of the past as well as newer understanding of emotional needs.

Of course, every increase in the power of the community to intervene, challenge, and investigate will threaten parental rights. On the other hand, every increase of parental power will lessen the ability of professionals (and others) to insist on protective intervention and supervision. In the end, children often need to be protected from both parents and professionals, particularly when they both agree on some suppression of a child's rights. Children have to be given the status of persons within the meaning of our Constitution. There

---

25 Katz, *op. cit.*, p. 17.
26 Gil, *op. cit.*, pp. 18–48.

are too many atrocity stories of juveniles being denied their basic civil rights and consequently incarcerated on the authority of one professional opinion with a parent's permission. Parents can also fight any outside intervention, and there are even more distressing stories of children who are returned to their natural parents and subsequently killed or maimed. Finally there are cases in which adequate parents have had children taken away from them because they deviated from the community's very narrow or very middle-class standards of morality. Usually the more visible poor will be challenged and become the subject of state intervention;[27] middle-class child abuse is more rarely brought to light. Institutionalized child abuse in overcrowded underfinanced schools, hospitals, and child-care centers completely escapes the public conscience. For how long?

When and if the movement to raise our consciousness in regard to children's liberation and children's rights gains ground, there will be much to review in our parent-child politics. If we truly put a high priority on children's physical and emotional welfare in this society, there would be many new developments. Legislation would be clarified and constructed with a consistent concern for the civil rights of children re institutions, professionals (including the courts), and parents. The rash of local laws punishing parents for their children's misdeeds[28] seems based on outmoded ideas about the reality of parental control and the state of family life. Such scapegoating of parents also militates against viewing the child as an individual who is not an extension of the parent's person or property. The rights of minors to privacy and health care become crucial in questions of drug treatment and contracep-

[27] Katz, *op. cit.*, pp. 22–51.
[28] An example from the New York *Times*, December 20, 1972, "Camden Law Makes Parents Liable for the Delinquent Acts of Children." Included was a clause calling for parents to enforce the city's 10 P.M. curfew for youths up to eighteen years old.

tion. All concepts springing from the private-property view of children should give way to a view of each child as a primary human trust, a trust which will determine our future society's well-being. Effective programs would have to be founded to support all parents, help parents who are in trouble, and substitute for parents who fail. The most delicate and difficult problem would be deciding on criteria for intervention and devising methods of supervision which would not seriously curtail liberty.[29] At present the most crucial and formative years of a child's life, from birth to six, can pass by in total privacy. After a birth certificate is filed, the community demands nothing and gives no help until school age is reached. The most pressured exhausting years of parenting, which also have the most potential for good and harm, are left completely unsupervised and unsupported. Only in a crisis are the rights of the powerless child considered.

One proposal which may herald a positive new direction is to establish a child advocate, or ombudsman, to represent the child, and only the child's welfare, in every local community. Could not a public guardian represent each minor child's interest to equalize the vested interests of parents, schools, police, hospitals, courts, welfare systems, and even child protection agencies? To institute a public child advocate would be to substitute a formal public protector for the informal protectors which used to be more effective in stable, traditional communities of interwoven families and professionals. It would be an embodiment of the idea of parens patriae, an effort to emphasize child-centeredness, to strengthen the powerlessness of the child's estate. As older children are given more of a say in custody cases, in either divorce, adoption, or child abuse, they need a voice dedicated solely to their interest,

[29] Morton Bard and Joseph Zacker, "The Prevention of Family Violence: Dilemmas of Community Intervention," *Journal of Marriage and the Family* (November 1971), pp. 677–82; Katz, *op cit.*; Gil, *op cit.*

more trained in knowledge of child development and family life than the average judge or lawyer. (Could older children formally fire their parents?) Western justice has always provided a disinterested third party when a powerless participant is involved in a serious decision. If, for instance, a professional such as a doctor, lawyer, or psychoanalyst is engaged and paid by adult parents, then they may not be disinterested. Parents and parental-type institutions are by definition interested parties, hardly capable of neutrality.

At the same time that children's rights and interests are newly supported, there's also a need to support and aid parents in their impossibly demanding job.[30] It's still another way to help children, as well. Family allowances, health insurance which guarantees medical care for a family, housing benefits, unemployment insurance, and more and better education programs will help parents be better at parenting. Parental education programs in the schools, churches, and other media of instruction, along with parent apprenticeships, and family centers would prove the community's concern and support for child rearing. If neighborhood family centers included day-care and other family-centered programs run with parent power, there could be enough variety and freedom for pluralistic values. Unfortunately, many people feel caught between justifiable fears of too much state power and intrusion into private life and a fear of too little social support for parents and children.

At this point in our society when we find ourselves trailing every other Western country in social guarantees and support of family life, I think we could dare to risk some of our vaunted individualism, privacy, and independence which also correlates with our soaring rates of child abuse and family breakdown. Facing a crisis in parent-child relationships, we have to do something besides mouth nineteenth-century rhetoric. Parental

[30] Bronfenbrenner, *op. cit.*, pp. 120–66.

failure and family breakdown are costly. The erosion of parental morale, and that internal legitimacy and social confirmation every person and institution needs to function well, is subtle but corrosive.

In an age of specialization, professionalization, and special interests, parents and children get ignored. The happy assumption that all is well in the private sphere of family life is blindness. What has heretofore been assumed as a stable background of our social life is an area filled with conflict, confusion, and uncertainty. In the end, if we don't give parent-child politics a high priority on the culture's social agenda, we are going to pay an enormous price. Parents are failing for many multifaceted, complicated reasons, but our individualistic ethic lays blame upon parents without delving any deeper or taking action. Today our children suffer from the breakdown of protective and supportive bonds, but tomorrow we all will. Faced with new dilemmas, we ask again the most fundamental questions: Are parents born or made? Do you learn to be a good parent?

Are Parents Born or Made?:
Sex and Learning

Some of the hardest questions about parents and parenting involve nature-nurture questions about human beings. Are parents born or made? Does sex make a difference? And is the general population with its culture more important than individual parents? Clearly, from my previous chapters, I take the position that individual parents are mediators of the general population, and that psychocultural shaping dominates the development of man. If so, sexual identity can be subordinate to the parenting role: Neither men nor women are innately better parents, or distinctly different socializers, unless cultural learning makes them so. I also see the course of past evolution to be a positively patterned influence on the present (committing the genetic fallacy and showing myself as a developmental optimist all in one blow). But once we reach man's privileged estate, higher than the primates, lower than the angels, the psychocultural cognitive factors mostly govern man's progress. The symbiosis of culture and nature becomes inevitable, and a good thing.

I see the development of parenting in evolution as a progress toward bonds of deep emotional and social commitments. The genetic population and the social structures of the group are affected by and in turn affect parenting processes. The rise of population thinking which looks upon each individual as embedded in a group has been inevitable since the Darwinian revolution.[1] Although Western individualism has always resisted granting the influence of the group, genetically and socially the population is more important than the individual. In the slow processes of evolving life, the interdependency of life upon life is crucial. Purposeful or not, the evolving story can at least be traced backward.

As far as we know, all cells issue directly from other cells; life comes from life, even when the old organism only splits in two. Still in these earliest stages of the simplest forms of life, one could say that new life is dependent upon pre-existent life. Dependency (at least temporarily) is certainly one basic characteristic of any new organism. Indeed, as evolution progresses and forms of life become more complex, we see a corresponding increase of the dependency of new organisms upon their procreating predecessors.

Although at the beginning of life's history dependent interaction is minimal, sexual reproduction appears and establishes a new process in which one comes from two. The two may hardly get together, at that. Fertilization of the eggs in the sea may be the only interaction of the parent fish with one another or with the new organisms. This laissez-faire form of external sexual fertilization is a wasteful and dangerous procedure when compared with the more efficient development of internal fertilization by copulation. In a further stage, reptiles could still more efficiently re-create the sheltering sea within an egg, and so become land animals. They could lay fer-

---

[1] Ernst Mayr, "The Nature of the Darwinian Revolution," *Science* (2 June 1972), pp. 981–89.

tilized eggs and hide them, so that the zygotes could have time to develop, break out fully formed, and fend for themselves.

Unfortunately, leaving a new organism to fend for itself in the presence of biological enemies is also a thoroughly inefficient way to survive. A lack of parental protection during immaturity leaves a young organism too vulnerable. A major evolutionary advance is seen in the development of the placenta and viviparity.[2] How much more efficient it is when a fertilized egg and its nourishment can remain dependent and protected within the mother until it is older and less vulnerable. In mammals, maternal nourishment of the young, with its increased parental protection from predators and starvation, insures a still higher survival rate and longer developmental period for the young. One can trace in the change from the open sea to hard-shell egg, to placenta, viviparity and nursing, an organism's growing independence of the general environment coupled with a growing dependency of the young upon parental protection. The method of reproduction is a form of protection insuring survival.

The aptly named "diligent parenthood"[3] of the higher species, especially among the primates, encourages more complex development in the young. A great deal of learning takes place through the contact and intimacy of adult feeding, grooming, and caretaking of the young. By and large, primate socialization and group living have been biologically adaptive for mutual defense, and foraging when there is an adequate food supply. The pooled capacities of the primate groups which can be shared through forms of social interaction is what makes the primates "primary" in comparison to their competitors. Adaptive learning and primate "culture" of a sort are inextri-

[2] Charles Kaufman, "Biologic Considerations of Parenthood," *Parenthood: Its Psychology and Psychopathology*, E. James Anthony and Therese Benedek, eds. (Boston: Little, Brown & Co., 1970), pp. 3–55.
[3] *Ibid.*

cably bound up with the parent-young relationships and group socialization. Some observers maintain that infants are the focal points of some primate social organizations.[4]

Clearly, among the primates social interaction, especially between mother and infant, creates differing bonds of affective relationships. These bonds are acknowledged by all those who study the primates. Apparently, a pair-bond between mates occurs rarely, an affiliative bond between adult female primates is more usual, but the mother-infant bond is universal. But what exactly is a "bond"? As students of primate social organization define it, "the term 'bond' includes only social relationships between specific individuals based on the performance of mutually reinforcing activities in addition to mating behavior."[5] For instance, in the different species of monkeys it is mutually reinforcing to regularly groom and greet each other, huddle together, and have communal nestings. In other words, bonding in primates must include more than the physiological interaction of sexual mating or mammary feeding. Such bonds involve complex preferences, affect, and social relationships which favor social learning and primate culture. The mother-infant bond is crucial.

But how do we get from primates to man? Although many serious students of primate behavior deplore the fact, primate studies gain their present popularity from our specifically human interest in the origins of the human species. Yet we know that since man and ape separated some 5 million years ago, few easy answers about human nature will be forthcoming. For that matter, not enough is yet known about primate social organization in the wild. Primate colonies set up by scientists in captivity are a priori subject to highly artificial conditions.

[4] *Ibid.*, p. 14.
[5] J. F. Eisenberg, N. A. Muckenhirn, and R. Rudran, "*The Relation between Ecology and Social Structure in Primates*," *Science* (26 May 1972), p. 864.

Despite these reservations, the fascination with primate studies continues. When psychologists adopt infant monkeys and raise them in human homes (with diapers, bottles, and toys) and try to teach them language communication, perhaps the rest of us can be forgiven for jumping too precipitously from monkeys to men. It may be inevitable in arguments over the differences between man and other animals to look at our nearest relatives in the animal world. At some point in the past we had a common ancestor, but with what common social characteristics is a matter of dispute. Primitive tools, teeth, thigh bones, and reconstructed skulls don't tell us much about the development of language, culture or, more to the point, protohuman parenting.

Enough is known now, however, to begin to outline a probable story. There seems to be major agreement that the process of evolving into man was a slow cumulative, interacting process in which few characteristics can be labeled completely distinctive or exclusively human.[6] Tool use, for instance, which was once thought to be a distinctive mark of man, has been found in chimpanzees in the wild. What remains distinctive and certainly human is the combination of many interrelated characteristics in a high degree. As usual in evolutionary questions it is difficult to tell what is cause and what is effect in the circular relationships. What seems clear is a simultaneous development of several interrelated changes. Among these developments, parenting becomes crucial and supremely important in the evolution of man.

Coming down from the trees and adapting to the plains, anthropoids began to walk on two feet. The development of the feet and hands meant that walking on two feet freed the hands for more extensive tool use and for carrying an infant

[6] Sherwood L. Washburn, "Aggressive Behavior and Human Evolution," *Social Change and Human Behavior*, George V. Coelho and Eli A. Rubinstein, eds. (Maryland: National Institute of Mental Health, 1972), 21–39.

too young to cling by itself. By contrast, monkey infants have to be born with a nervous system advanced enough to be able to cling to their mothers who still need their arms for locomotion. With an anthropoid walking upright and using tools, there was both a smaller birth canal and a selection for larger and larger brains. The adaptive solution was an earlier delivery of infants in a more immature and helpless state. This immaturity and incomplete development of the nervous system which required more parenting, more contact, also involved more learning and increased cultural socialization.

The slow growth and helplessness of the unfinished human infant assure the huge part caretaking plays in man's development, what Bruner calls "the uses of immaturity."[7] As the dependent period is extended and mutual interaction between adult and infant is intensified, so is the affective bond and learning by observation. Caretaking, contact, intimacy, and time for communication, play, and social learning are extended in a long infancy and childhood. With a larger brain at work, increased memory, recognition, and a future time sense increased the affective bonds. The need to co-operate for defense, foraging, and preplanning other activities for survival developed language, still the most superb human facility. Language is possible because of the development of the human brain, palate, vocal chords, and so on, but surely its use increased self-reflection, reasoning, co-operation, and more creative invention. With language, abstraction from the concrete is possible; the freedom to manipulate symbols must have aided human beings manipulate the environment to survive. From the beginning human dominance and survival were tied into communication, co-operation, and affective interdependency.

Parenting the young increases in importance. Following the evolutionary pattern, the greater dependence upon parents is

[7] Jerome S. Bruner, "The Uses of Immaturity," *Social Change and Human Behavior, op. cit.,* pp. 3–20.

correlated with greater independence of the environment. T.
human infant is the most helpless living organism, but through
parental protection and socially conveyed learning, the even-
tual master of the earth is created. Parent-child interaction
links prehuman and human life; and human parenthood is distinctive from primate parenting in crucial ways. But tracing the
exact evolution is difficult. The origin of the family has been
hotly debated for centuries, even before primate studies, anthropological investigation of primitive societies and theories
of evolution appeared. So many crucial issues are involved, particularly the relations between the sexes, the division of labor
and the nature and role of women.

It is at least certain that sexual changes took place. Human
sexuality is not as limited as primate sexuality by endocrino-
logic domination. Human females are free to be sexually recep-
tive all the time, even as they live beyond child-rearing age.
An increase in female sexual receptivity accompanied a decrease
in the indiscriminate sexual intensity which among primates is
said to interfere with parenting: "The sexual mania during
estrus interrupts normal social behavior and interferes with the
care of infants."[8] With decreased intensity, more cerebral control, and increased spans of receptivity females could have
longer spans of improved child rearing without loss of sexual
activity. A sexual bond between male and female could be
strengthened so that parental functions could be better carried out. A permanent pair-bond controls continual sexual
competition and the social disruptions attendant upon sexual
promiscuity. At the same time the human mother, who while
carrying her infant is unable to move rapidly or fight, can profit
from male protection and male foraging and hunting. Stable
sexual bonds facilitate male-to-male co-operation and group co-
hesion, as well as parenting.

[8] Kaufman, *op. cit.*, p. 16.

Already in primate society there is some division of labor based on gender and the beginnings of a generalized fatherliness which complements the universally strong and specific mother-child bond.[9] In early human societies, pair-bond parenting with specific fathering probably evolved as more adaptive, despite earlier theories of primitive group marriages. With the development of language and cognition, affectual and sexual ties beyond a concrete present are possible. Long-term bonds and rules for inhibiting sexual and aggressive behavior develop with the social organization of family and kinship groups. Kinship ties, food sharing, and a home base of co-operation are very basic to social organization. Of course, dating these developments is difficult; one expert concludes rather tentatively:

> I am myself inclined to think that family life built around tool use, the use of language, cookery and a sexual division of labor, must have been established sometime between about 500,000 and 200,000 years ago.[10]

Complementary organization of sexual pair-bonds into households and families with offspring meant that fatherhood, at least social fatherhood, became specific. If fathers did not recognize their own biological procreative role in producing their offspring, at least they recognized them as their family and entered into an affective social bond. The mother-child bond became expanded in human parenthood into a mother-father-offspring bonding. The advantages to human offspring of having two protective parental adults are obvious. A two-parent sexual division of labor made possible an increased dependency and longer development of the human young.

[9] Eisenberg, Muckenhirn, and Rudran, *op. cit.*
[10] Kathleen Gough, "The Origin of the Family," *Journal of Marriage and the Family* (November 1971), p. 764.

Among humans a mother-child relationship is never unaffected
by the sexual pair-bond; even the absence of a father is significant. Fatherhood, social or biological, is an all-important
formative influence, yet to this day the importance of the father
has been underestimated in studies of family life.

A negative male mystique has operated in theoretical investigations of present and past social organization. Males
have certainly held power and oppressed women and children
in many recorded historical civilizations (Old High cultures),
but these cultures may really in the long run be a minority of
all human experience. The excessive imbalance of male power
in the high civilizations which formed our own cultural perspective may have made us misread our own past and other
primitive societies. The picture of a brutal aggressive cave man
terrorizing his fellows, subjecting women against their will, kill-
ing his fellows indiscriminately, and despoiling the earth may
not be accurate. Primitive man as a bloodthirsty hunter who
uses the male hunting group to dominate the earth may be a
projection into the past of present-day obsessions with power
and aggression.

Some investigators of early man and the evolution and diffusion of culture have questioned the idea of early man as first
and foremost a hunter. By observing the most primitive existing societies in which gathering is primary and hunting a secondary source of food, they conclude:

These facts suggest that gathering, rather than hunting, was
the first major subsistence activity of human beings. This
finding, if true, overturns the now popular view of early man
as a bloodthirsty caveman, whose adaptive success was due
to his interest in weaponry combined with a calculated feroc-
ity. Like our nearest relatives, the great apes, and like
present-day gatherers, early human societies were probably

nonaggressive, highly intrasupportive teams of foraging ama-
teur botanists, quarterbacked by women and guarded by
males.[11]

Obviously it is still a moot point whether the meek inherit
the earth. Dominance in man may be quite a different thing
than dominance in animals, having more to do with inhibition
of aggression. Anthropologists like Lionel Tiger and Robin
Fox (the name and game are the same) may roar forth theories
of the biological dominance of aggressive males, all to no effect.
Survival in humans may go to those who outwit and outnur-
ture the competition.

It may also be true that male-female relationships throughout most of man's existence as a species have been more equal
and complementary. Women played an important role in early
cultural development and the equal economic and sexual division of labor did not give men oppressive power. Neither
men nor women could survive long without the work and produce of the other sex, so stable matings were encouraged. Kathleen Gough, an expert on matriliny, claims that women in a
society have more power and independence when they produce food rather than when they simply process male-produced
food. Yet even in hunting societies women have dignity and
power; "there is reciprocity rather than domination or exploita-
tion."[12] Greater male strength and mobility give men an edge
in public authority and rank, but then society is still simple,
with no state or concept of private property.

The imbalance of power between the sexes arises with a
more complicated productive society where there is excess
wealth, inheritance of property, and social stratification in a
state. According to Gough:

[11] A. Lomax with N. Berkowitz, "The Evolutionary Taxonomy of Culture," *Science* (21 July 1972), p. 234.
[12] Gough, *op. cit.*, p. 768.

With the rise of the state, because of their monopoly over weapons, and because freedom from child care allows them to enter specialized economic and political roles, some men —especially ruling-class men—acquire power over other men and over women. Almost all men acquire it over women of their own or lower classes, especially within their own kinship groups.[13]

At this point in cultural evolution, when sexual divisions of labor became separated from productive equality, then reciprocity, interdependence, and equality between men and women suffer. It would be interesting to correlate, if possible, whether parental roles and parental power also change with male dominance. A ruling class may look upon children as a means to continue dominance (through inheriting property, power, status) rather than as fellow members of a band dedicated to survival. I would see the status and fate of women and children as entwined; the suppression of women spells the suppression of the child. In humans the parental relationship reflects the marital relationship in many political and psychological ways. Unequal power between males and females in the family affects a child's model of the world.[14]

But feminists who posit an ancient original matriarchy are mistaken.[15] In the earliest cultures, which have existed during most of man's time on earth, stable pairing and vital complementary work of men and women meant mutual respect and mutual dignity. It is important in present controversies over sex and parenting to remember that marriage and the family

[13] *Ibid.*
[14] Ronald V. Sampson, *The Psychology of Power* (New York: Vintage Books, 1968); and William J. Goode, "Force and Violence in the Family," *Journal of Marriage and the Family* (November 1971), pp. 624–36.
[15] Elizabeth Gould Davis, *The First Sex* (Baltimore: Penguin Books, 1971).

long antedated class inequality and male sexist oppression. The
family is more uniquely human. As Kathleen Gough notes:

The family is a human institution, not found in its totality
in any pre-human species. It required language, planning,
cooperation, self-control, foresight and cultural learning, and
probably developed along with these.[16]

For thousands upon thousands of years the family was the
major organizational principle of society, the base of much creativity, bonding, and cultural progress. The family arose because man was human (no matter how many million years it
took), and the family made man distinctively human.

In fact, parenting still makes a human being human. If baby
monkeys cannot do without mothering,[17] the individual human infant is in a far worse state. Humans, who are born far
more helpless as infants, have far more to learn. The unfinished
neonate is just beginning on his voyage to human adulthood.
But contrary to past misconceptions, the helpless infant is no
tabula rasa, waiting for any and all cultural conditioning and
learning. Inheritance from our past human history cannot be
discounted. Earlier theorists of parenting and child rearing believed in an empiricism and behaviorism which asserted that
only what went into a child came out of a child. Experience
and learning were the only determiners of human nature.

For some reason this learning-theory approach was supposed
to be an optimistic doctrine and identified with a belief in the
future and progress. The point was, I guess, that proponents
of the tabula rasa approach felt that parents, caretakers, or
teachers could with education erase all past human failings. In
one generation, no less! Human heredity was a minor consider-

[16] Gough, *op. cit.*, p. 769.
[17] Harry F. Harlow, "The Maternal Affectional System," *Determinants
of Infant Behavior* II, ed. B. M. Foss (New York: John Wiley & Sons, 1963).

ation and environment was everything. All human learning and ideas were built up through associations and connections. Whether the mind was visualized as a blank tablet or a black box, the important thing was to get the right stimuli in so that the correct responses came out. Watson, the cheerful behaviorist, believed that he could take any baby and produce doctor, lawyer, or Indian chief.

Arguments about the primacy of nature versus nurture have raged back and forth in intellectual circles. Today the proponents of heredity and genetic determination are staging a comeback. Arguments about the relationship of race to inherited intelligence are at the center of one current debate. Inherited temperamental patterns and genetic make-up are another. Interesting questions, but at this point debate still has to be conducted with rudimentary measurements and crude understanding of the variables which go into human development. After all, we have only the barest beginnings of an understanding of the interaction of heredity, human cognition, emotions, and environmental influences.

As the psychologist Anne Anastasi says, the wrong questions have been asked for too long.[18] Instead of asking how much is heredity and how much is environment, or which trait is inherited or which learned, we should be asking how heredity and environment interact. Environmental influences can begin within the womb with the nutrition of the mother, or the effects of disease radiation, drugs, or other prenatal influences. Heredity, from conception on, interacts with environmental factors, with the different outcomes affecting all future outcomes in development. At each stage there are several possible outcomes which shape future possibilities. There may also be

[18] Anne Anastasi, "Heredity, Environment, and the Question 'How'?" *Readings in Child Development and Personality*, Paul Henry Mussen, John Janeway Conger, and Jerome Kagan, eds. (New York: Harper & Row, 1965), pp. 5–20.

sensitive periods in human development when certain environmental experiences can affect inherited capacities more than at other times. Animal studies have shown that early imprinting, a special form of learning in which inherited readiness and environmental factors coincide, is irreversible. Some early experiences in childhood and infancy may be similarly influential in consequent human development.

Anastasi speaks of a "continuum of indirectness"[19] in the influences upon behavior of hereditary factors and organic environmental influences such as birth injuries or prenatal nutritional inadequacies. Such indirect influences may then affect other direct immediate influences in the environment which can be "best conceptualized in terms of breadth and permanence of effects . . . a continuum of breadth."[20] An example of a broad immediate environmental factor would be membership in a social class.[21] The influence of class-distinct economic factors and interpersonal styles in the family and home can affect other developments in a child. For instance, reading readiness in first-grade children may be related to styles of parent-child interaction since verbal communication is much more encouraged and practiced in middle-class families. But even within a class there are numerous other cultural factors which can also make a difference.

The complexity of human development is overwhelming. There are so many variables interacting in each unique individual's heredity and life situation. The very richness of normal human capacities and the different dimensions of development make it more confusing. Unlike fruitflies, rats, or rhesus monkeys, we know that human beings can and do simultaneously develop physically, cognitively, musically, artistically, morally,

---

[19] *Ibid.*, p. 8.
[20] *Ibid.*, p. 11.
[21] Melvin L. Kohn, "Social Class and Parental Values," *Readings in Child Development and Personality, op. cit.*, pp. 345–66.

and emotionally. Indeed, there may yet be untapped human resources. It is also apparent that many, many people do not fulfill even a minimum of their known human potential. The more we know about the potential of man, the more impressed we are with the wastefulness and distortions in human life.

All is not chaos, however. For many infants born, there is an average expectable environment (i.e., parents) which nourishes and gives the new organism the environmental releasers it needs to develop. The use of the term "environmental releasers" shows my adherence to the theory that there is an ordered developmental sequence or life cycle ready to unfold in the human organism. Without certain stimuli and certain minimal conditions, growth will not take place, but the impetus for growth is given in the genetic make-up of human beings. We cannot make our children grow any more than we can make plants grow, though we can starve both. Human growth progresses as one level of development builds the base for the next. Timing and rates of growth may be quite uneven, with spurts of growth taking place and plateau periods in between, but the sequence is generally ordered.

We know more about children's development because this century has been blessed with great explorers of the subject. Giants such as Montessori, Gesell, Piaget, and Erikson have pioneered in child studies. There are many differences between the different theorists, but the idea of an ordered developmental sequence in a favorable environment is common to almost all. Rough norms for different age groups exist, so that ages of walking, talking, certain measures of motor co-ordination, certain levels of intelligence and other capacities can be predicted.[22] There are individual differences, to be sure, and parenting can make for differences, but there is enough conver-

[22] A. Gesell and F. G. Ilg, *Infant and Child in the Culture of Today* (New York: Harper Bros., 1943).

gence to ensure norms. Some knowledge of these norms and patterns of growth helps parents.

An instructive example involves language acquisition. It appears that after much study of different children learning different languages (thirty languages or so have been studied), regular patterns are followed.[23] At first the child can only say one word, usually a proper noun, or the name of some familiar object he sees every day. Then according to researchers at "about two years—give or take a few months—a child begins to put two words together to form rudimentary sentences. The two-word stage seems to be universal."[24] At first the children with their two-word limit, bound by a reliance upon action and the immediate context, depend upon intonation, word order, and inflection to get their message and meaning across. They make up the appropriate combinations themselves, creating new combinations which could never be simple imitation of adults. Such creative speaking is generally not concerned with remote possibilities or might-have-beens, for early language reflects the small child's concern with the here and now— location, action, and immediate personal needs. Language is embedded in action.

From two-word combinations, a child proceeds to three-word-limit combinations in which a lot of meaning has to be crammed. The child wants to say more than he can manage linguistically. Gradually each preschool child masters the incredible task of learning to express his meanings in an expanded form with his language's basic grammar operations. "They all are acquired by about age four, regardless of native language or social setting. The underlying principles emerge so regularly and so uniformly across diverse languages that

[23] Roger Brown, *Social Psychology* (New York: The Macmillan Co., 1965), "Language: The System and Its Acquisition," pp. 246–349.

[24] Dan I. Slobin, "Children and Language: They Learn the Same Way All Around the World," *Psychology Today* (July 1972), p. 73.

they seem to make up an essential part of the child's basic means of information processing. They seem to be comparable to the principles of object constancy and depth perception. . . . There are linguistic universals that seem to rest upon the developmental universals of the human mind."[25] The use of language follows certain developmental principles which correlate with developing cognitive capacities.

Jean Piaget, the great observer of Geneva, has done years of research and writing on the stages and ages at which a child can perform certain reasoning tasks or come to certain logical deductions. Things which adults take for granted were once mastered by the small child when he was ready. The child only gradually learns to assume that objects and relationships exist apart from himself and his own immediate perceptions (achieving object constancy). In the thought of the child, a "decentering" of the world takes place along with an expansion of the time sense.[26] It takes until adolescence for the development of abilities to handle abstract, formal reasoning tasks. When symbols can be manipulated, an adolescent can begin to reason without being bound by immediate, concrete, self-centered perceptions.

Piaget sees that the growth of cognitive intelligence is reflected in the language of the child and also in the moral reasoning of the child.[27] In moral development also, a decentering from childish egocentrism and his own point of view begins so that a child begins to be committed to rules, fairness, and ideas of justice. There is an evolution of moral consciousness in which ideas of responsibility, including autonomy, reciprocity and intent, are grasped as important. For Piaget, there are two different moralities that the child follows, one with adults

25 *Ibid.*, p. 74.
26 Jean Piaget, *The Language and Thought of the Child* (New York: Humanities Press, 1959).
27 Jean Piaget, *The Moral Judgment of the Child* (New York: The Macmillan Co., 1965).

and external authorities (rules of constraint), and one he follows with his peers and playmates (rules of mutual agreement and co-operation). Piaget thinks that co-operation through autonomy is not only more effective but much superior; it accords with an inherent thrust of the developing child.

Piaget maintains that just as there is an innate developmental scheme in intellectual growth, so "It cannot be denied that the idea of equality or of distributive justice possesses individual or biological roots which are necessary but not sufficient conditions for its development."[28] While the idea of punishment has psychobiological roots, and jealousy, sympathy, and reciprocity appear early, none of these will develop without social organization and the experience of living and playing with others. In playing a game of marbles, for instance, small boys are easily trained by older boys in respect for the law because "they aspire from their hearts to the virtue, supremely characteristic of human dignity, which consists in making a correct use of the customary practices of a game."[29] For Piaget the good is no Platonic ideal but is taken as "a form of equilibrium immanent in the mind."[30]

Other psychologists have developed similar interpretations of individual moral development. Lawrence Kohlberg[31] has outlined stages of ongoing moral development in individuals from seven to seventeen and beyond. The successive moralities are not taught but develop in the individual as over-all capacities and experience increase. The move is toward autonomous conscience and freedom from external authority and rules, but also includes a concern for the good of the social group. It is a long, complex, subtle development which in some ways parallels the

[28] *Ibid.*, p. 318.
[29] *Ibid.*, p. 21.
[30] *Ibid.*, p. 385.
[31] Lawrence Kohlberg and Carol Gilligan, "The Adolescent as Philosopher: The Discovery of Self in a Postconventional World," *Daedalus* (Fall 1971), pp. 1067–86.

development of language and thought. Another unique developmental human characteristic in which parents co-operate, but do not have to create on a tabula rasa, solely from scratch! In getting all this together, Erik Erikson, the psychoanalyst, has put forth perhaps the most inclusive developmental scheme.[32] He tries to synthesize physical, social, cognitive, emotional, and ethical human development. He calls his developmental scheme epigenetic, to emphasize that every stage is built upon the previous one and contains the past within it. "In an epigenetic development of the kind here envisaged each item has its time of ascendance and crisis, yet each persists throughout life."[33] Each stage involves genetic factors, social factors, including strong parental influence, and the development of the individual ego. The individual is always dependent upon the matrix of social organization within an ongoing cycle of generations.

Erikson wants to emphasize the strengths of man, so often ignored in psychology's concentration on pathology. He proposes the existence of an evolutionary adapted schedule of human virtues which are developed in childhood and adulthood within the life cycle; these are "integrated psychosocial phenomenon." As he succinctly states it at one point:

> I will, therefore, speak of Hope, Will, Purpose, and Competence as the rudiments of virtue developed in childhood; of Fidelity as the adolescent virtue; and of Love, Care, and Wisdom as the central virtues of adulthood. In all their seeming discontinuity, these qualities depend on each other. . . . Also, each virtue and its place in the schedule of all virtues is vitally interrelated to other segments of human development, such as the stages of psychosexuality

[32] Erik H. Erikson, *Insight and Responsibility* (New York: W. W. Norton, 1964).
[33] *Ibid.*, p. 140.

which are so thoroughly explored in the whole of psycho-analytic literature, the psychosocial crises, and the steps of cognitive maturation.[34]

I find the idea of an interrelated physical, moral, intellectual, and psychosocial development convincing. It's no accident that intense heterosexual-love experiences develop in adolescence. The body's sexual maturing is matched by the development of abstract reasoning when symbol use and a decentered cognitive point of view become possible. Heterosexual love is possible when one can seek and participate in the opposite sex's world, relatively freed from a child's concrete egocentric constraints. Physically, intellectually, morally, and socially an individual becomes ready for a new dimension in life. But still, the study of developmental stages is too rudimentary.

Yet who wants to quibble with the pioneer investigators of human development? Of course, they disagree with each other, and in many aspects their own arguments are open to question and further work. Too little has been done on man's musical-aesthetic-religious human development, for instance. And more to the point, parental development has not been enough studied. But the concept of normative, ordered human development has gained credence. Everything is not permissible, nor is everything possible in shaping human development. Parents find themselves starting with children not in a void, in a vacuum, or with a blank slate, but rather within a long ongoing process of human evolution over generations. Parents have an ally within each child which urges growth. Humans, like animals, have been biologically prepared over a long past to learn some things easily (like language); and these learning experiences progress in sequential development. The developmental sequences in our peculiar species include complicated interactions of psychocognitive factors and sociocultural environ-

[34] *Ibid.*, p. 115.

mental factors. Man is different from other animal life in his complexity, capacity, consciousness, and conscience. His aspiration toward goals and values beyond the concrete means that human horizons are high, wide, and distant. Parenting is a form of midwifery to a remarkably complex and subtle process of development.

Those who study human development now have to take full account of each individual as a complex psychosomatic unity. Once it was progress to prove that human behavior could be affected by physiological causes, instead of demons, sin, or cursed fate. Slowly, Western man came to accept germs, epilepsy, syphillis, malnutrition, and genetic disease (among others) as causative factors. But this concept of organic disease so thoroughly won the day that the idea of psychic factors affecting physiology was almost dismissed. Having once emerged from the mire of superstition, science avoided recognizing psychic or emotional factors in illness or human development. Under the reign of runaway empiricism, ethical, religious, and value discussions were equally tabu.

But today, when computers have made cognitive studies respectable, brain waves can be measured, and drugs induce altered states of consciousness, science has expanded its horizons. Human consciousness has begun to be studied seriously.[35] In one such study of the physiology of meditation, measures of brain waves, respiratory rate, and skin resistance of the meditative stage in yoga practitioners were taken.[36] The results of meditation were found to be different from those of wakeful activity, sleep, hypnosis, operant conditioning, or fight-or-flight reactions. "The pattern of changes suggests that meditation generates an integrated response, or reflex, that is mediated by

[35] *Altered States of Consciousness*, Charles T. Tart, ed. (New York: John Wiley & Sons, 1969).
[36] Robert Keith Wallace and Herbert Benson, "The Physiology of Meditation," *Scientific American* (February 1972), pp. 84–90.

the central nervous system."[37] This may be the opposite of the fight-or-flight reaction. The investigators speculate that in man's evolution what was previously adaptive for survival may not now be adaptive in our complicated stress-filled environment. Of course, those concerned with infant survival and parent-child interaction may feel that incessant defense-alarm reactions are never adaptive and never have been.

Studies of optimal human development and the part played by psychic factors in parent-child relationships have also been made scientifically respectable by work with primates and rats. What psychoanalysts and other suspect scientists could never "prove" with people can be shown by experimenters with a primate colony at their disposal. (Whether the worm-runners can ever catch up is anybody's guess.) At any rate, concepts such as parental love, care, bonding, enriched experience, and rejection are beginning to get concentrated attention. Long before infant monkeys were deprived of mothering, or kept in the dark to produce depression and retarded bone development, perceptive observers noted that human babies in foundling homes seem "to become sad and many of them die of sorrow."[38] Subsequently, within the last thirty years or so, more exact observations of emotional deprivation in children began to ascertain the effects of unhappiness. The studies of many such as Bakwin, Ribble, Bowlby, Spitz, and Wolf concurred in the conclusion that separation from mothering, or inadequate mothering, produced biological and psychological damage to the infant. Deep depressions and withdrawals were observed in babies; grieving children were listless, apathetic, failed to gain weight, despite adequate nutrition; they were also prone to respiratory infections and fevers. Infants in foundling homes

[37] *Ibid.*, p. 90.
[38] Lytt I. Gardner, "Deprivation Dwarfism," *Scientific American* (July 1972), p. 76.

had a high death rate, and if they did survive, often showed severe physical and mental retardation.

Infants "fail to thrive" if given inadequate mothering and an impoverished environment. Emotional hostility to an infant and child can physically affect his development. A student of "deprivation dwarfism"[39] investigated the mechanisms by which emotional attitudes can even affect a child's growth. While many abnormally short children may have lesions of the pituitary gland or some other organic condition, some "thin dwarfs" are reacting to disordered family environments. A child of fifteen months who was kept isolated and unattended in a dark room was lethargic and severely retarded in growth. Removal to a children's hospital and "a normal emotional environment" produced dramatic changes in growth, weight, and social responsiveness.[40] These effects have been reproduced many times; some children have even been hospitalized, recuperated, returned home to suffer recurring retardation, and then come back to the hospital to gain weight and grow. A case of twins in which a mother rejected the male twin after her husband's desertion was particularly convincing. The normal and equal growth rate of the twins changed from the time of the desertion so that "from the 15th week onward the boy's growth rate fell progressively behind his sister's. By the time he was a little over a year of age his height was only that of a seven-month-old."[41] This child, too, recovered with hospitalization and with the restoration of the parents' marriage caught up with his sister.

Lytt Gardner, the investigator, theorizes that emotional disturbance may affect the endocrine apparatus: "Impulses from the higher brain centers, in our view, travel along neural pathways to the hypothalamus and thence, by neurohumoral mech-

[39] *Ibid.*
[40] *Ibid.*
[41] *Ibid.*, p. 78.

anisms, exert influence on the pituitary gland."[42] Besides exhibiting bone-age retardation, these children show an upset hormone balance, perhaps resulting from abnormalities in their sleep. An adverse emotional climate has also been shown to suppress appetite in adolescents and to halt menstruation in girls. These clues to the interrelation of the different brain centers may point to a "series of differing, age-mediated physiological responses to what are essentially identical psychosocial stimuli."[43] Since the "psychosocial stimuli" in question produce a suffering child, Gardner and others who study the effects of emotion on child development are participating in unfortunate experiments of nature. You cannot equal unhappiness for a demonstration of "the delicacy, complexity, and crucial importance of infant-parent interaction."[44]

But the basic idea of parent-child emotions having such an effect on growth was put forth long ago by one of the early psychoanalysts, Georg Groddeck. He maintained that if the wish to be big were not present in each child, "We should remain small and never grow. Or do you think I am deceived in thinking that there is a certain connection between people's remaining little and their wanting to be little . . . that the not-growing tall arises from the wish to have an excuse to be still a child?"[45] In 1923 Groddeck's belief in the psychosomatic unity of man seemed eccentric; it was not then possible to measure growth hormones in the blood, or so exactly observe sleep patterns and bone age. (Nor had infant monkeys been reduced to complete depression, or executive monkeys been given ulcers, or rats used to prove the effects of psychological factors upon physiology.) Only human intuition and keen observation gave

42 *Ibid.*
43 *Ibid.*, p. 81.
44 *Ibid.*, p. 82.
45 Georg Groddeck, *The Book of the It* (New York: Vintage Books, 1961), p. 189.

the pioneers in psychoanalysis an accurate grasp of the psychosomatic unity of the human organism.

Still, for parents and others who want to know the extent of the psychocultural versus genetic influence, frustration awaits. The interaction, or to use an even stronger term, the fusion in man of cultural and biological elements makes it almost impossible to separate one from another. In fact, parents in producing and rearing children provide a prime example of the absolute fusion of culture and biology. They provide the new organism's unique heredity by uniting their own biological inheritance, but from conception on they are a primary force in the environmental factors which influence both biological and psychic development. Finally, parents transmit to the child their own particular variant of their group's culture. Naturally these influences interact in circular ways. Nor should we underestimate the child's influence upon his parents as individuals, as a couple, and as members of society. At this point we would have to say that rather less than more is known about these complex interrelationships.

To make a guess displaying my own bias, I would say that heredity and physiological factors can be the primary determiners of an individual's developmental destiny only when it is grossly deviant from group norms. Idiocy, severe physical deformities, incapacitating genetic disease will provide an overwhelming organic determination of human development. But if inherited genetic characteristics are in the range of normal or above, then psychosocial stimuli will be the primary factors in an individual's development. Still, confusion comes from the fact that in every different situation various degrees of interaction of physiology and psyche will have different results. There are always the neglected, deprived children who do not die in foundling hospitals. Many children in families with both parents mentally ill grow up unscathed while tenderly mothered infants develop childhood psychosis. Why is it that some children can overcome severe disadvantages while other children succumb? Our inability to make accurate predictions reveals a fundamental lack of knowledge. The same complexity and ignorance handicap our understanding of parental development.

When we talk of a parental instinct, we mean a complex learning produced by a combination of psychobiological and cultural factors. Probably, some inherited innate thrust to survive, to reproduce one's own kind, to mate sexually is entwined with an experientially produced need to love, to live in a caring group, to gain status as an adult, to identify with one's parents and reproduce social reality. During the millions of years of man's evolving, biocultural evolution has selected for altruistic parenting. As we have seen, the origin of the human family and the origin of human species are intimately interconnected. The earliest and strongest bonds exist between parental caretakers and the infant; the infant develops, indeed must develop, within a positive emotional relationship of mutuality and interdependence. Understandably, in a normal human life cycle, man in adulthood reaches a generative stage (Erikson) when one can generate, care for, and sustain the next generation— just as one was once cared for. Having been parented, one aspires to parent. Maybe this altruistic parenting desire includes an aggressive seeking of restitutive power, or a strategy to increase one's kind in dominant ascendancy; but if so, it is adaptive in coping with reality. Successful parental protection and nurturing of offspring require active effort, self-confidence, and dominance over the environment, as well as thinking and feeling.

If we maintain the primacy of psyche and learning in man, then when we ask whether sex determines parenting, we can say that neither males nor females are innately programmed to parenthood nor do they inherit distinct styles of parenting. The move from primates to the human species was built on the expansion of the mother-infant bond to include specific father-child ties and the importance of learning in the transmission of behavior. Parenting is mostly learned from identification with models. Unfortunately, when parenting was first studied intensively, the inevitable tendency of psychoanalysts and other researchers was to concentrate attention upon the mother as *the* influential parent. Since our nineteenth-century Western civilization was one of private individualism, with mother and child isolated at home, observers minimized the influence of fathers, peers, or the larger society represented in the social network. The fact that every mother had been influenced by her mother was recognized, but other social influences upon mother-child interactions were minimized.

Anna Freud herself, who believed it *demonstrated* "that all advantages of a later family life may be wasted on a child who has lacked a warm and satisfying mother relationship in the first instance,"[46] could still give warnings against overworking the mother's influence. In a discussion of the concept of the rejecting mother she says:

> Whether owing to the fault of the analysts who were too emphatic in their statements, or owing to the fault of psychiatrists and caseworkers who were too bent on exchanging a multitude of causes of mental trouble for one single, simple, causal factor—the idea of being rejected by the mother suddenly began to overrun the fields of clinical work and casework.[47]

Everything from autism and psychosis to mental retardation was pronounced the result of a rejecting mother. Anna Freud believes a rejecting mother is a serious problem, but she cau-

[46] Anna Freud, "The Concept of the Rejecting Mother," *Parenthood, op. cit.*, p. 376.
[47] *Ibid.*, p. 377.

tions against forgetting that "no degree of devotion on the part of the mother can successfully cope with the boundless demands made on her by the child."[48] Every mother who is the first representative of the external world will inevitably appear somewhat frustrating and rejecting to every child. As Anna Freud very sensibly says, "We the observers must not share the infant's delusion."[49]

Nor need we as present-day observers share a full-blown psychoanalytic point of view or the nineteenth-century cultural context in which it flowered. In today's culture, do male and female sexual identity have to be given such a prominent part in preparing for parenthood? The received doctrine has been quite sure that male and female parents should play quite different roles in the development of their male and female children and that females are innately better prepared than males to play a nurturing parental role to the human young. Anatomy is destiny, particularly for females. Believers in innate mothering responses assert that female hormonal systems program women for maternal behavior; acculturation and social influence are secondary to heredity. In the psychosomatic unity of the organism the soma is more in control when it comes to female reproductive behavior. Sexual hormones in the developing fetus re-enforce genetic sexual inheritance and program the brain for future female, or male, behavior.

Some observers have felt that while human sexual identity and mating behavior are subject to cultural and social conditioning, maternal behavior is biologically programmed and unvaried. As David Levy, the student of maternal overprotection, says: "It may be true that the maternal drive, a drive so basic to survival, has a higher degree of resemblance in man and animals than does the sex drive. Certainly there is a remarkably close resemblance of the criteria of maternal care used in our

[48] *Ibid.*, p. 385.
[49] *Ibid.*

study in all mammalian behavior. The sexual life of man may
be determined by psychic and cultural influence to a much
higher degree than the maternal life."⁵⁰ The theory is that
maternal behavior is more basic for survival and has a powerful
"endogenous nature" which is related to female aggression and
hormonal influences. Variations in maternal behavior among
young girls are constitutional; those with aggressive and helping tendencies from childhood are more naturally maternal,
made so by innate biological factors as well as social and psychic
influences. In this theory a distinction is made between feminine behavior and maternal behavior; very "feminine" women
are not good mothers because of their passivity and lack of
aggressive dominance.

It is also thought that the hormonal influences, or programming for female-male sexual attraction, are different from maternal behavior. According to some experts, there is a behavioral
correlation with the presence of the hormone prolactin during
the later half of pregnancy, as well as from the pleasure-
sensation-causing hormone oxytocin which appears at birth.⁵¹
Maternal nursing and caring for the infant give relief and pleasure and create attachment and mother-infant bonding. Others
maintain maternal development also reactivates a female's
vaginal libido,⁵² which was the source of primary motherliness expressed by little girls in doll-play. Maybe. But everyone
championing biological programming still admits that culture
and social conditioning can suppress, distort, and interfere with
these female biological predispositions. Also innate male programming for parenting is rarely posited or studied. A few
iconoclasts have maintained that men are the more nurturing
sex, since they have spearheaded reforms in child rearing, child

⁵⁰ David M. Levy, "The Concept of Maternal Overprotection," *Parenthood, op. cit.*, p. 408.
⁵¹ Lucy E. Cutler, *Scientific American* (April 1972), p. 6; and Therese
Benedek, "Motherhood and Nurturing," *Parenthood, op. cit.*, pp. 153–65.
⁵² Benedek, *op. cit.*, p. 156.

care, and pediatrics. After all, is not primate fathering more generalized, including all of the troop's offspring?

What can we make of these complicated questions? First of all, the use of animal analogies is a double-edge sword. One can use the maternal-deprivation studies of primates to show not innate programming but the need of early social experience to develop adequate motherliness. Even in primates physical contact and the female infant's social interaction (play, grooming, huddling, clinging) are as important for mothering as hormonally controlled behavior. Maybe the study of maternal behavior follows the law that the more that is known about any animal behavior, the less purely biological and innate it seems. If social learning and particular experience are important for maternal skills among animals, how much more so among human beings. Surely, the most important factor in human mothering is a woman's social acculturation and learned understanding of her physiological female potential.

The physiological differences between males and females, which probably include activity levels as well as metabolic and hormonal differences, always must be mediated through culture. There may be a critical period for learning our sexual identity (a form of imprinting or easy learning), so that experientially we are set as males or females and sexually and socially oriented. A developing male or female body confirms the evolving social-sexual identity and role learning. A process of "self-categorization" as a male or female takes place.[53] If the original sociosexual identification does not, for some unusual reason, match the body involved, the learned sexual identity or imprinted gender role appears stronger. Social learning shapes sexual development.[54] Penis envy may only occur in little girls when males have an enviable edge in social life; or

[53] L. Kohlberg, quoted in B. G. Rosenberg and Brian Sutton-Smith, *Sex and Identity* (New York: Holt, Rinehart & Winston, 1972), p. 82.
[54] Rosenberg and Sutton-Smith, *op. cit.*, "Resolution," pp. 79–90.

womb envy in little boys may be correlated with uncreative or threatening male roles.

When we come to parenting roles and parent-identifications, even more sociocultural factors may be at play than biologically programmed maleness or femaleness. Both males and females may aspire to giving, protecting, and nurturing since they have both been parented. The active aggressive component and tender, loving components (instrumental and expressive) needed in nurturing the young may be highly developed in both sexes through identification with their parents and other parent figures. If men have seemed more nurturing and caring, it would be because socially they had been given more nurturing, more care, and more powerful wherewithal to aggressively protect the young. Similarly, the young female's tendency toward doll-play and nurturing roles could quite easily be explained by the fact that she identifies with her mother and quite correctly deduces that her own biological potential includes the capacity for childbearing. A smart three-year-old can figure these things out, perhaps even without vaginal libido.

Not that we should ever underestimate the power of a woman's pleasure. Since most physiological functioning does give pleasure in a sensual-social way (if not severely repressed), it's no surprise that childbirth, nursing, child care are sensually reinforced by pleasure in addition to social status and esteem. Niles Newton has written of the "trebly sensuous woman"[55] in order to emphasize the pleasures involved in childbirth, and nursing, as well as orgasm. Female sexuality may be more extended in time than male sexuality as well as more intense (but it may be slower to be aroused and mature). Feminine interest in infants and maternal roles can be a conscious reasonable search for a social-sensuous fulfillment of distinctive female

[55] Niles Newton, "The Trebly Sensuous Woman," *Psychology Today* (July 1968).

sexual potential, deduced and learned but not innately programmed.

The strength of cultural influences and learning is such that
I am sure that a society could very effectively suppress or sub-
limate women's desires for childbearing and child rearing. So
too, cultural influences could suppress the parenting desires of
males. Already, men living with an older male ideal which does
not allow tenderness, expressive emotions, or playfulness are
able to suppress their own identification with childhood and
care giving. Since men do not identify with their mothers so
closely and identify more with fathers who are usually removed
from full-time parenting, it may be easier for them as a group
to renounce parenting. Even so, varieties of personal temperament and personal experience within a particular culture will
determine how strong the urge to parent will be in either male
or female. Human parenting is far more personal than sexual.

Social experience shapes hormonal or inherited sexual determinants because evolution of the human brain has so pro-
gressed that it is consciousness' psychic, abstract, cognitive
mediation of physiology which determines our deepest desires,
emotions, and aspirations. In the past our inherited biological
potential and our social organizations have been united in a
more or less harmonious whole, adapted to surviving in the
environment. The adaptive fit of culture and biological reproduction has led us to think more things are organically fused
than they are in fact (for instance, the identification of female
maternal behavior and mating behavior which may be quite
different). In a changing culture, as in artistic creation, things
which have always been linked together can be separated—or
things which have always been divided can be coalesced into
new wholes.

In the future most of the arguments about parenthood will
be about how far man can stretch or separate from his adapted
past without serious psychological alienation and social mal-

function. Right now our new concern with ecology and environment has taught us the dangers of discounting the existing interrelationships of nature. At the same time the population crisis has convinced us that more intervention and control of "natural" parenthood is necessary for survival. Nature doesn't always know best.

Parents, finally, mediate biological inheritance and the psychosocial conditioning and stimulation known as culture. While heredity and culture interact in crucial ways, cultural conditioning is usually dominant; in man the higher brain centers can interpret and control internal stimuli as well as manipulate the external environment.

Man is different from the animals in the primacy of his social co-operation, cognition and emotions, and his resulting mastery of nature. While parenting among the primates may display many of the same functions as in man, the processes are different and far more complicated in man. There is little so-called parental instinct or innately programmed mothering or fathering. Human parents must learn to parent, they must be self-conscious. With man, cultural learning is crucial, and in parenting culture is transmitted. Recognizing the primacy of culture, however, does not begin to solve the problem of deciding which cultural values to choose. With our future sense intact, we have to consider where we are going. What of future parenthood?

Future Parenthood

What of future parenthood? Many of the current reapprais-als of parenthood involve predictions and prescriptions for the future. Regularly we can read challenges to the continuing ex-istence of "the family as we know it," or even to the biological processes of sexual reproduction which we have developed over the millennia. The birth announcement of a test-tube baby is eagerly awaited along with the demise of individual parents in favor of group rearing.

What are we to make of these floating forecasts of future parenthood? With the advent of asexual reproductive tech-niques, will women (and men) cast off the "bonds of biological animal procreation"? Will socialization of children be sepa-rated from their physical procreation since, in the words of one feminist, "there is no inherent reason why the biological and social mother should coincide"?[1] Can we substitute in-novative reproductive techniques and communal child rearing for the biologically based individual parenting of old?

Unfortunately, those who propose changes and predict new

[1] Juliet Mitchell, *Woman's Estate* (New York: Pantheon Books, 1971), p. 119.

forms of procreation and parenting rarely follow through with detailed analysis. The test-tube baby advocates and those who wish to abolish the family hardly ever get beyond the first radical steps. Ideologically they leave the babies on the laboratory's doorstep or vaguely talk of providing "a serene and mature socializer"[2] for each child in some sort of communal context. What's usually missing in these discussions is a recognition of the long-term commitment required, or that follow-through parenting in middle childhood, adolescence, and young adulthood has an important function. Old age is also ignored, of course; being ushered into life has no reciprocal connection with ushering one's parents out, when all ideas of overlapping life cycles are ignored.

But the ties that bind the generations are swaddling bonds, necessary for continuity. Present parenting is connected to past parenting and affects what can be evolved in the future. Those making efforts to reform, substitute for, or scrap an institution like parenthood have to understand the potency of present practices. I would contend that the positive attributes of man are so dependent upon parenting as it has evolved in the species that we have few options for change. We would end up, in any future, reinventing parents and the family; if parenthood did not exist we would have to invent it.

In other words, man the inventor, creator, master over nature, who thrives by interfering and changing the environment, is himself first shaped by patterned interaction with caretakers. There may not be any such thing as a parenting instinct, but pragmatically parents and parenting functions have been, are now, and will be necessary for each newcomer's survival in the group. Indeed, the group population is more important than the individual; yes, learning and culture are far more important than biological unlearned responses, but that doesn't mean we

---

[2] *Ibid.*, p. 146; also, David Cooper, *The Death of the Family* (New York: Pantheon Books, 1970).

can go directly to asexual reproduction and group child rearing. Individual parents need to remain as biological and cultural mediators of the group for one all-important reason, often left out of ideological rearrangements of society.

If the last thing a fish could discover is water, so it is with man's emotions and feelings; they are the most important things that man has to take into account in reinventions of reproduction and socialization. Without attachments, bonds, desires, fears, and repugnancies, human life would hardly be possible. The unemotional life is not worth living. Positive and negative emotions are totally adaptive for survival as a species. Not only must one fear danger but also have a will to live. With distortions and flattening of affect and emotion, human beings do not care enough for themselves to maintain life, much less to mate and reproduce. "Cold" cognition will not do; it takes "hot" cognitions or emotions to initiate and sustain the activity of living.

This is all obvious, of course, but well worth thinking about again when considering future utopias and basic changes in human beings. Human emotion is a complex fusion of thinking and feeling in which self-consciousness and body reactions also fuse. In human beings you must have both conscious awareness and a body, since neither could have evolved without the other. The psychologists, playing around trying to develop "emotional" computers with "hot" cognitions, have their work cut out for them. Developing sense receptors is a lot easier than getting a biochemical endocrine system together on its own two feet. Somehow, self-consciousness is inimitably tied to mobility,[3] body consciousness, and bodily experience, as the distressing unresponsiveness of the corpse attests. Whatever the state of the body-mind problem in solving the relationship of

[3] Silvan S. Tomkins, *Affect, Imagery, Consciousness: The Positive Affects* (New York: Springer Pub., 1962), p. 10.

bodies and minds, a human being functions and feels in an embodied set up, complete with emotions.

My contention is that parents give us both our bodies and our self-conscious emotions through procreation and caretaking. Even our own body image is formed to a great extent by incorporating another's perceptions of our bodies. Along with our mother's milk we take in her point of view. Interactions through touch, eye contact, kinesthesia, and auditory stimuli give us a social body-self, to fuse with the physiological organism.[4] But more important, parental caretaking releases emotional attachments and patterns emotional reactions. With an infant's limited perceptual equipment and attention span, a strong, deeply emotional attachment can be made with only a limited number of involved caretakers (one, two, three at most?).[5]

Moreover, the bonds that build up through early social experience seem very specific. From general social responsiveness the baby moves to specific emotional preferences in his attachments, and these are generally parental. Being specific about preferences is a mark of a higher organism. Monkeys get fairly specific in their bonding behavior, and man even more so. It's no accident that the more an organism is dependent upon learned social behaviors, the more specific and strong its emotional attachments. We could say that the more brainy, the more emotional, along with extended dependency periods upon a specific parent-newborn tie.

In the past, internal gestation and live birth in an immature state have made our species dominant. Large brains, long learning periods with slow maturing have given human beings the

---

[4] Sidney M. Jourard, *The Transparent Self: Self-Disclosure and Well-Being* (Princeton: D. Van Nostrand Co., 1964), "Body Image, Spirit, and Wellness," pp. 91–98.

[5] H. R. Schaffer, "Some Issues for Research in the Study of Attachment Behavior," *Determinants of Infant Behaviour*, II, B. M. Foss, ed. (New York: John Wiley & Sons, 1963), pp. 179–99.

malleability and adaptive creativity to subdue the earth. This evolutionary development, traced in the previous chapter, has been based upon social learning during a long dependency upon parents. First of all, sexual reproduction was adaptive as a protective mechanism for the young; and diligent parenting provided further protection after birth. Bonding between primate monkey mother and child was expanded in humankind to mated pair bonding and progeny bonding, known to us as family ties. Sexual reproduction and parenting, given human potential, becomes involved with love, loyalty, pride, and long-term mutual commitments (as well as conflicts and possessiveness).

The point is that physiological sexual reproduction, emotional ties, and social parenting are all fused in human parenting. The care-giving and care-soliciting behavior necessary for group survival from one generation to another are embedded in emotional bonds cemented by sexual mating and reproduction. In a real way the family is overdetermined; social learning, emotional bonding, and survival as individual and group go together. Adaptive socialization and reasoning ability develop along with deep emotional ties of parent and children. The long years of protective caretaking that each human infant requires to become independent are better guaranteed by parental emotional involvement with the ensuing sociocultural organization of kinship ties and obligations.

The question we must deal with now is how our human past predetermines what we can do in the parental future. To what extent can man intervene and put asunder what adaptive evolution joined together, and with what effect? Biological parenthood and social parenthood have been one and the same, but must it be so? Take for example the most glaring and obvious exception, the case of adoption. In adoption a person, or persons, adopts a child who is not their own biologically procreated child. With this social-legal commitment, full responsibility of parenthood is granted and accepted, along with all inheritance rights for the child. In other words, complete social parenthood can be a matter of will and commitment, irrespective of and beyond biological parenthood.

Many peoples in diverse places have had the custom of adoption; it was quite frequent among our own American Indian tribes. Indians adopted not only Indians but any kidnaped white children. Many white children who were adopted into Indian families became more Indian than their new families, proving the dominance of culture over race. Several fierce chiefs who fought against the white settlers in the 1700s were born "white." For their part, the first white Americans also had a tradition of adopted sons and daughters, a custom long established in Western civilization. Christianity even has as a central tenet each believer's adoption as a son of God. Mere birth, or birth order, is secondary to being chosen as heir with new sisters and brothers in the Lord.

But it is well to remember, whether in primitive or high culture, that adoption was still an exception which conformed to the norm and imagery of sexual reproduction and biological parenthood. The model which governed the practice was one in which conception and birth govern kinship. Adoption rites aim to produce a blood brother, to bring forth new believers from the womb with much labor (St. Paul's words), to reproduce the irreversible biological ties of the family. Today when adoption has reached new proportions in American culture, spurred by generosity, affluence, and population concerns, we can see cases of conflict between biological and social parents. The courts are called to decide whether the rights of "natural" parents take precedence over the rights of adopted parents. In tragic cases foster parents fight biological parents for custody, and vice versa.

Racial loyalty and ties of blood have also entered the adoption picture. Many black groups resent the growing practice of interracial adoption. Parents who adopt children from a different race feel an obligation to make them proud of their own racial heritage. They can no longer ignore genetic and biological parentage. Many adopted children also show curiosity about their biological parents. A conflict of interest arises when adopted children become adults and demand that adoption agencies provide confidential information so they may trace their natural parents. The courts then have to deal with these claims and the counterclaims of adopting parents who understandably feel that they are the "real" parents of their adopted children. From the point of view of adopting parents, the biological facts of parentage are hardly relevant when compared to social parenting.

Surely in a direct conflict and forced choice, sociocultural parenting is more important than biological parenting, more real in the long run; but physiological conception and birth are also important and not simply insignificant. An adopted child's curiosity about his biological parents is based upon a realization of the importance of biological inheritance in overlapping generations. When coming into adulthood, or preparing to give birth, or even upon seeing one's children grow up, or as parents approach death, a consciousness of biological continuity and the organic dimension of life becomes important. Parents normally mediate both biological life and sociocultural personhood and when these roles are split, there is a felt difference, a discomforting discrepancy.[6]

This difference between functions does not necessarily cause harm when and if the sociocultural parenting is done well. The commitment of adopting parents to protect, nurture, and socialize can with love successfully graft the new branch onto the tree. But the norm is still there. The adopted child is "just

[6] Marshall D. Schecter, "About Adoptive Parents," *Parenthood: Its Psychology and Psychopathology*, E. James Anthony and Therese Benedek, eds. (Boston: Little, Brown & Co., 1970), pp. 353–71.

like" the child of one's loins, or the child of one's womb. Emotionally and legally the child is incorporated or placed in the ongoing family and the blood ties of grandparents, aunts, sisters, brothers, etc. The specificity and willed commitment of parenting *can* be emancipated from the biological parenting; the emotional bond can be forged without blood ties, but the norm remains an irreversible physical relationship completed by irreversible social commitment.

The inherent connection between physiological parenting and social parenting lies in the sharing of a specific almost identical past (genetic inheritance line), sharing the intimacies of gestation, birth, and nursing, and the irreversibility of having this specific child. Normally, physiological sharing, closeness, and irreversible physical relationship support parental empathy, affection, intimacy, and commitment. The physiological conditions predispose behaviors which protect and nurture an infant as they produce a deepening emotional bond.[7] Since each parent has once been through the developmental drama and learned all the parts, parenting roles come easily. But the physiological processes put us on the stage and select the scene and cast with which the all-important psychological dimensions will interact.

Some of the same predisposition to self-love and self-involvement which begins with our embodied physiological existence is invoked by physiological procreation. Our lives are entwined with those lives we produce, just as they were entwined with those who produced us. While this involvement can be denied and forcefully suppressed, or worse still, be negatively deformed, it still does seem to be a biocultural fact.[8] Indeed, even a positive tone, an altruistic pleasure in the bonded parental involvement seems ascendant as a norm.

[7] Lucie Jessner, Edith Weigert, and James L. Foy, "The Development of Parental Attitudes During Pregnancy," *Parenthood, op. cit.*, pp. 209–56.
[8] John Bowlby, *Attachment and Loss* (New York: Basic Books, 1969).

Otherwise the group would not have survived. When an anthropologist finds a tribal group such as the Ik,[9] a people who sunder every positive bond and suppress all empathy, he finds a group already starving, disorganized, and on the way to extinction. Even the infamous Ik raise their children for three or four years before rejecting and casting them out. They may abandon the old, laugh at each other's misery, and attack and steal from each other, but infants must have some parental exemption from misery to insure minimal group survival.

Of course, our future problems are not that of a primitive marginal group reduced to barbarism by starvation. We are struggling instead with the options of affluence and technological mastery. Our self-questioning is whether our human abilities to intervene and control life will reduce humanizing conditions. So far I have reasoned that adoption can be positively humanized, but that it follows the norm of biological parenthood. The controlling intervention here is like a transplant engrafted in the body without danger from immunological reaction. Positive human emotions and easily reproduced bonds of caring parental involvement give life to the technique. It is a truism to say that intervention and technology can be at the service of man, as well as "take over"; but I am willing to define "taking over," in questions of future parenthood, as any situation in which emotional ties and bonds are very likely endangered.

Naturally, this view is based upon a value system that sees the goal of evolution to be positive human emotions and caring bonds between human beings. I agree totally when Ashley Montagu says that the ideal of human-to-human behavior is modeled on a mother's loving treatment of her newborn dependent infant:

[9] Colin M. Turnbull, *The Mountain People* (New York: Simon & Schuster, 1972).

. . . the whole course of human evolution has led to the fact that human beings shall relate to each other as a loving mother relates to her dependent child. Such relatedness has had the highest selective value for the human species in all societies and in all times.[10]

Furthermore, I think in our long history such altruistic pleasure in mutual human exchange and presence has made man what he is. Only a most blind and disassociated intelligence could fail to see man's need not to allow technology, control, or intervention to distort the elementary ties and primary bonds of parent and child.

On the other hand, I do not share the current disenchantment with medical progress which blames all our problems on man's new mastery over nature, but adheres to the traditional Western view of the potential goodness of rational control. Human technology is a triumph with innumerable benefits to us all, individually and as a species. The positive aspects to our human nature's efforts to control and better life are worthy of respect.[11] Future parenthood will benefit from developing techniques of parenting, biologically and socially. Technological control and intervention in nature can help humanize and encourage parent-child bonds and positive attachments. Recognizing that there can be good technology and bad technology, it is easy to see a good technology's role in helping present and future parenthood.

Fertility control and techniques for improving childbirth are examples of technical intervention which serve parent-child bonding. Contraception can channel and focus parenting so that more parental time, energy, emotion, and resources can

[10] Ashley Montagu, *Man Observed* (New York: G. P. Putnam's Sons, 1968).
[11] René J. Dubos, "Humanizing the Earth," *Science* (23 February 1973), pp. 769–72.

be given to each child. Birth control is the counterpart of the technical reduction of infant mortality. As man controls the death rate of his young, he also controls the birth rate (with considerable lags here and there). Basically, birth control will be a precondition of all future parenthood; contraception will become more effective and as routine as giving babies injections to insure immunity to diseases which used to cripple and kill. No people who have seen their infants die of whooping cough or smallpox have to be persuaded that it is better to have shots and to vaccinate. So too, all groups facing starvation or a decline in maternal health or family disorganization will be persuaded of the benefits of routine voluntary contraception, when it is perfected and available.

Also, the interventions and techniques for prenatal care and childbirth that the educated affluent now possess will in the future be sought for everyone. Proper vitamins, diet, medical supervision, and childbirth techniques are other benefits of a good technology. In another instance, the growing medical specialty of "fetology" extends man's technical assistance to the fetus in the womb. Amazing feats of *in utero* transfusions and operations have been performed and will be performed as knowledge increases. While such exceptional interventions will always be rare, a day-to-day improvement through the development of knowledge can be expected. The most knowledgeable and sophisticated techniques, perhaps, involve psychically and physically training women themselves to control and manage their own childbirth.[12] To teach a woman consciously to control a normal childbirth is a far more inventive and effective means of control than the crude bludgeoning techniques of drugging and forceping, cutting and stitching, etc.

The resources of the psychosomatic human organism have

[12] Pierre Vellay, M.D., *Childbirth Without Pain* (New York: E. P. Dutton, 1960).

just begun to be explored. In normal childbirth it is all to the advantage of the process to have positive conscious co-operation of both parents so that the psychophysiological process can be fully experienced. Here the techniques of education, conditioning, and training serve positive emotional involvements, humanizing the beginning of the parenting process. In a way, the joyful peak experience of conscious controlled birth (falsely called "natural" birth) is a model of technical rational control of a physiological process. The physical and mental techniques involved strengthen the active involvement of the parents, as well as benefit the physical health of mother and baby. The emotional bond between parents is strengthened when the husband prepares with his wife and helps in the birth. Having a happy birth experience of accomplishment and active purpose (often painless) gives a positive imprint to initial parent-child relationships. The baby gets more oxygen and more positive affect, each equally important in life's beginning.

The sophisticated psychophysical education and techniques involved in conditioned childbirth processes should apply to all of man's control of nature and himself. The point is to enhance and deepen an already adaptive psychobiological process. Man should control through co-operation with and through the human organism, a control which does not deform, or destroy, but may transform a biological process. Drastic intervention, mutilation, substitution are reserved for emergencies and an extreme life or death situation. Such a view of intervention and good technology stresses co-operation with what is and has been in the psychobiological environment. The past informs our present state as much as our future. Some of our worst natural and social disasters on earth have come about through arrogant disregard of the environment, both physical and social. Man's obsession with power, his demand for a com-

plete submission to his will, has been destructive.[13] We have
learned to mistrust the thrust for absolute control in any area
of life. So in reproductive processes we seek an ecological approach aiming for a flourishing land rather than a dust bowl.
We would control our reproduction and parenting by adapting
to its adaptive functions, respecting our inherited bodies and
emotional reactions as much as our reasoning ability. For future parenting it is vital to understand that man's social nature
makes our communal ties and interactions as important as the
individual will.

Future parenting in my opinion has to avoid two opposite
dangers and destructive trends. One is the growing tendency
for parental control and reproductive technology to turn children into manufactured products; the opposite danger lies in
the continuing diminishment of parental rights and functions
so that parent-child ties and emotional bonding and nurture
are flattened and subjugated to the group (i.e., the totalitarian
state). In the United States, individualistic overcontrol is
more of a danger. The individualism which informs our culture already tends to view a child as a form of private property.
So far, only in adoption-agency procedures, mandatory school
attendance, and extreme child abuse (when it is detected)
are there any checks on parental decision-making. Surely parents who wished to have a child "made to order" would have
a good chance of procuring any available technology.[14] At this
time artificial insemination with anonymous donors takes place
so that women who want to have a child may do so. Currently,
sperm is stored in sperm banks for the purpose of artificial insemination. In the future, there well may be sex determination

[13] "One may well want to reconsider the relationship between the will to
master totally, in any form, and the will to destroy," Erik H. Erikson,
Young Man Luther (New York: Harper Bros., 1964), p. 108.
[14] Paul Ramsey, "Shall We 'Reproduce'?: I. The Medical Ethics of In
Vitro Fertilization," *The Journal of the American Medical Association* (June
5, 1972).

of offspring and techniques for transferring embryos from one womb to another, or to artificial wombs. Eggs may be fertilized in laboratories and finally asexual reproduction techniques with one parent perfected (cloning). Scientific experimenters with these technologies invariably give as their rationale that they are trying to help parents (or a parent) in their desire for children, or for a certain sex, or for optimal children.

The argument for advancing all reproductive technology is based upon man's rational nature and his right to intervene and control events to the betterment of all concerned. Granted, technology is natural to man; his ability to survive is founded on his intervention and control of nature. So why stop at reproduction and parenting? As Joseph Fletcher, the moral theologian, puts it, "A 'test tube' baby made artificially, by deliberate and careful contrivance, would be more *human* than one resulting from sexual roulette—the reproductive mode of the sub-human species."[15] The question of course is whether man's good penchant for technique can become excessive and destructive—"deliberate contrivance" of what, for whom?

It seems clear to me that there is a reproductive Rubicon which is crossed when man's technical intervention changes from a positive to negative effect. Just as certain kinds of over-kill technology ruin the land, the forests, the waters, air, and animal life, so good reproductive technology can become dangerous. The taking-over line is crossed when artificial intervention in adoption, birth techniques, fetology, and contraception begin to serve the will and wishes of parents or powerful states rather than to better parent-child bonds, or serve the powerless child. Contraception, of course, can be said to serve only an adult, but then there will be no "parent" or new life involved. When a developing life is or will be involved, should

15 Joseph Fletcher, "Ethical Aspects of Genetic Controls," *New England Journal of Medicine* (September 30, 1971), pp. 5–6.

technology be used simply to impose parental wishes and will? I say no.

Consider the case of women who want to be pregnant so much that they are willing to have artificial insemination with the sperm of anonymous donors. They have doctors who use reproductive technology to serve the woman's individual will and wishes. Their husbands, the anonymous donor, the child, are not served. An individual doctor who employs the technology also takes responsibility for the emotional effects on marital partners and on parent-child relationships. The resulting legal squabbles still remain to be clarified, but more significant will be a thorough investigation of psychological factors in all parties concerned. Why do not the donors feel as responsible for the use of their sperm as they would of their words, or possessions? How do physicians deal with the genetic and other variables in making decisions? And how do children feel who find out they have been conceived in this way? What does it do to a marriage or family?

Of course, when the same technique is used to allow husband and wife to be successful in reproduction, you only serve the norm which has been adapted to emotional bonding. You do not disturb the context and configuration which leads to specific parent-child bonding and kinship ties. As in adoption, the biological norm is the mode and the two parents are *equally* involved. There is no inequality or disunity; either both are biologically reproducing or both are adopting through willed commitment. I do not think that an individual woman's desire to be pregnant, per se, should be served by technology. Nor, at the same time, should a woman's desire not to be pregnant with a child be served by the technology of the future. The possibility of artificial wombs and host mothers calls into question the status of pregnancy and the role of women in future parenthood. Pregnancy should neither be overvalued or undervalued to insure optimal emotional ties and female self-respect and dignity. Renting or giving womb service to another is a fragmentation of body-self which women have fought in prostitution, rape, concubinage, and the custom of wet-nursing.

Women have struggled to become whole persons whose bodies are not seen as a conglomeration of functions. The ancient Venus statuettes, in which female figures consisting of vulvas, bellies, and breasts, sans legs, arms, and heads, expressed a regressive and recurring view of women. To retreat to a point where woman's physiological functions were once again separated from her whole personal life and put at the service of others would be sad. Processes of pregnancy and birth are psychological personal preparations for parenting and attachment, not to be despised as subhuman. It is difficult enough emotionally, to give a newborn infant up for adoption in unfortunate circumstances; to institutionalize the practice and the corresponding disassociation of pregnancy and parenting would be degrading and dangerous.

For women to avoid pregnancy and seek artificial substitute processes would be self-rejecting. Such attempts define pregnancy as a burden and abnormal, a view of the human body which accepts the male version as the normal. Pregnancy is then given a negative evaluation, in the disease category, rather than as a valued good potential of women. It is important to get the right balance. Pregnancy and maternity do not complete women, or somehow automatically fulfill them or make them worthy (overvaluation). But neither is pregnancy a burden, a disease, or degrading animal function to be avoided (undervaluation). Pregnancy and childbirth, like sexual intercourse, are valuable, good physical processes which involve psychological consciousness, pleasure, and expenditures of energy. Only in exceptional circumstances is an adult or fetal organism unable to bear the stress of pregnancy. Artificial wombs and interventions in the pregnancy process should be reserved for those relatively rare circumstances when pregnancy is dangerous for a woman, or dangerous for the developing life.

Clearly, emergencies and exceptions are not the same thing as acceptable norms. The course of evolving parenthood has been toward two-parent bonded reproduction with in utero growth and extended dependency. The very method of reproduction insured protection and nurturing. In a way, artificial conceptions and artificial wombs regress to the reptilian-egg-in-the-sand stage of parenting with its attendant dangers. Who will care for these young, be protective of them, sustain the emotional care and commitment that long dependency requires? Eggs and glass placentas can be smashed or tampered with, even before the young emerge. Only specific parents protect from predators; the essence of human maternity and paternity is aggressive defense of the young. However, in the mammalian world, when maternal identification of her own young breaks down, maternal aggression is turned against the newborn animals. When an animal kills its litter or eats its young, it is because the female no longer perceives her young as young but as intruders who are not immune from attack. Intervention in the reproductive process can disturb normally protective mechanisms.

Now human beings are not lower animals when it comes to perceptual processes. But human protective mechanisms may still be affected and activated by a sense of possessive involvement. For instance, experiments on live fetuses have been performed after the fetus has been aborted and is no longer under parental protection.[16] Since the fetuses are destined to death, and rejected by progenitors, they are in the power of scientific experimenters. In the same way when parents implore or com-

16 "Research on Human Fetuses," *Journal of the American Medical Association* (November 2, 1970), p. 923; "Research on the Fetus," *British Medical Journal* (June 3, 1972), p. 550.

mission scientists to produce a baby for them artificially in the laboratory, the resulting embryo is beyond their protection. They and the embryo are subject to a third party's technical expertise. (The parents are even more removed than in cases of artificial insemination.) When a technician in a laboratory joins egg and sperm, the course of that developing life is beyond protective controls.

Perhaps even more dangerous to parental protectiveness is an attitude that children in a new technological era must measure up to some criteria, set by parent or reproductive technician. Such criteria-setting can only threaten the inalienable right of an individual to exist simply as a member of the human species. Picking and choosing among various levels of perfection or acceptability corrupt the parent-child relationship. The rationale for infanticide, especially female infanticide, always rests on the parental right to extinguish new human life which does not measure up. The right to choose and control for the optimum baby is inseparable from the right to destroy or eliminate undesirables, non-optimals. To order a wanted child to specification implies a right of rejection if the order is not filled. Infanticide is already being publicly debated as the next step in parental rights.

Sex determination of a child by its parents is not as drastic but is a related question. It is not just a problem of individual sex choices imbalancing the population. (The estimate that too many males would be chosen by parents is grossly distorted, I'm sure, but no matter.) The principle of actively controlling a child's individuality is more central. In such an increase of parental power and preference there is the suggestion that the child must accommodate the parent as an extension of his will, rather than the parent accepting and accommodating to the child as a unique inalienable individual. But there is a passive aspect to good parenthood, an unqualified acceptance and receptivity, which is important for human beginnings and the establishment of basic trust. As Jules Henry so perceptively says: "The assumption that whoever is wanted will necessarily be loved is false."[17]

Wanting a boy, or wanting a girl, already qualifies the preparation for parenthood, much less ordering a male or female. Sexual make-up should not be ordered for one person by another, any more than should eye color, height, I.Q., temperament, and so on. Psychologically, a child defined or ordered in its parent's image is in trouble. Preconceived (and here preconceived is a literal term) notions of a child as a perfect Gerber-baby girl or boy retard real parent-child accommodation and appreciation of unique babies. Inevitably too, as children grow up, separation and individuation have to take place. Both parent and child have to be weaned. I think this process is prepared for and prefigured by the unpredictability and uniqueness of the newborn. The givenness of this new human being, this other, may be a jolt but a healthy one. The sooner parents learn the primordial parental lesson, the better: It's not what parents *want*, but what parent and child can work out together. Each child is a new human being.

We get a totally unique new child thanks to sexual reproduction—a desirable characteristic of parenting. Asexual cloning by one parent reproducing his own genetic make-up would be disastrous. Sexual reproduction brings a unique new genetic combination into existence each time and this has been found to further the evolution of our species. The randomness and chance factors involved have been a source of creativity. In psychological terms the important sense of being a totally unique individual is bound up with the operation of chance, newness, and one-timeness in our make-up and history. To be a manufactured, ordered, produced genetic copy of one parent (albeit different in environment and developmental history)

[17] Jules Henry, *Pathways to Madness* (New York: Random House, 1971), p. 196.

would impinge on a sense of individuality and identity. If we value original paintings, first editions, handcrafted one-of-a-kind things, we should be able to see the importance of a unique genetic identity. Everybody a first- and last-folio edition, womb-rubbed and penis-crafted if possible.

Of course the right to be a unique new individual would not be invaded by good technology's interventions to cure genetic defects and disease. Man the master should work to conquer congenital defects such as heart disease, mental retardation, and all other heartbreaking birth defects. But bringing what is latent in an individual genetic heritage to fruition, or correcting crippling defects, is quite different from rationally manufacturing a genetic copy of a human being. It is the principle at stake as much as the incredible complications of who would make which decisions for whom. It is an aesthetic value decision as well. Personally, I would far rather be a chance by-blow of two sexually functioning people than a manufactured lab-produced copy of any one body. We need sex in our future for many reasons.

But an emphasis upon sexual reproduction is not the same as stressing sex differences. In future parenting and parent-child interaction, sexual differences may become far less important. The difficulties of raising a human being will be so complicated and involved that sex roles and stereotyped sexual functions will become peripheral matters. As each sex's stance in society broadens, with fewer economic and emotional complementary functions, there is even less reason to desire children of one sex or the other. Parenting becomes ever more unified and less differentiated, with fewer distinctions between a father's role or mother's role. The protective, partnering, nurturing, and launching roles of parenthood are much the same irrespective of sexual identities. Mothering and fathering coalesce into parenting, or rather, rise to a new level of complexity beyond sexual identifications.

Only a delight in sexual variety will remain, even though social sex roles are not polarized. Physiological differences in sex can remain emphasized by different gender displays which children learn by imitation of their parents and others. A feminine or masculine walk, gestures, facial and bodily postures can be learned or imprinted without being a sign of widely different social, economic, and familial roles. Sexual displays of sexual identity may be needed for courtship, coitus, and reproduction but not govern other aspects of life. Our society is and will be too complicated to be organized along sexual lines. Parents and children will find personal identity to be a goal which includes sexual identity only as a component.

Cultural recognition that parenting has coalesced into a unisexual activity spurs the acceptance of one-sex parenting. Single men or women can now raise their own or adopted children. It still isn't easy or ideal, since two parents give each other every kind of support, from financial aid to shared experience. But a particularly female or masculine experience of life is not crucial in good parenting. If the single parent is not rejecting of sex and sexual identities, the important central functions of parenting can be carried on effectively. Of course, when homosexuality is seen as abnormal, a rejection of the opposite sex and heterosexual relations, then homosexual parenting would be seen as distorting and damaging to a developing child.

Clearly, any sexual arrangements of a single parent are important since sexual partners need to have a positive nurturing (parental) attitude toward the children and vice versa. The jealousies and antagonisms which in a family are checked by mutual parental involvement can distort a single parenthood in which there are sexual partners but not parenting partners. Obviously, when two parents are bonded to each other and their children, it is a more protected situation. From the images of wicked stepmothers and stepfathers of fairy tales to current statistics on child abuse, one sees the lessening of protection for a sex partner's children, when a parental commitment is not assumed.

One of the challenges of future parenthood, in which we will see more and more mixed families (your children, my children, our children), will be to establish strong parental ties in confusing circumstances. Understanding the essential nature of parenting will help; as well as understanding that in human beings it is possible, if not preferable, to emancipate the emotional nurturing and commitment from the biological ties. The norm continues to be set and given vigor by the constancy of bonds arising from the traditional congruence of the biological and social. Traditionally, too, some operation of chance is important to guarantee a unique individuality in offspring who can then be better seen as separate beings with inalienable rights, separate but irreversibly linked. The possessive identification which comes from biological parenting also predisposes to empathy, emotional bonding, and altruistic involvement.[18]

I repeat. For the future I see only minor deviations from the biological norms of sexual procreation. No *Brave New World* or 1984 revolutions await us. The conservative, overdetermined nature of existing parent-child interactions precludes much future variation. Exceptions and substitutions into normal patterns may increase, but they will still tend to aspire toward the biological norm. I base my predictions of reproductive conservatism not so much on man's good sense, good will, or lessons learned from technologically induced disasters in nature, instead I count on the fusion of reproduction and psychological formation. In every human consciousness, emotional bonding has been built upon adapted reproductive processes and parental nurture. Since parental nurturing completes the nervous system's development and structures the perceptual emotional world of each newborn

[18] Norman L. Paul, "Parental Empathy," *Parenthood, op. cit.*, pp. 337–52.

who survives, a set is created in human beings to reproduce the cycle. There is a thrust toward sexual congress and parenting, as one has been parented. There are also, of course, many conflicting factors which may divert or suppress the impetus to parent and these will be much stronger in the future. Many more people will themselves choose to be childless, but they would not choose or allow radically different methods of parenthood for the rest of the population. I do not think parenting could be changed unless you could drastically break the cycle and in one generation impose a whole new method of reproduction and early child rearing.

That being unlikely, a radical break in continuity seems improbable in any foreseeable future. The technological possibilities in future reproduction will not be implemented when they do not serve the established norm. Instead, we may see attention turned to the psychosocial role of parenting, a deepening of parental commitment on the part of parents, and a raised consciousness of child-rearing responsibilities by the community at large. Population pressures and the felt need to limit the number of children born will facilitate a higher concentration of effort upon the rearing of fewer children. Future parenthood will be different, but different more in degree of intensity and required commitment. Quality issues will subsume biological innovation as psychological sophistication and social concern constantly increase.

If we avoid war, economic and ecological disaster, we shall gradually attend to our children as the chief determiners of our quality of life. After all, people pollute, people cause crime; violence and danger come from people. Barring a total collapse into decadence, which I seriously doubt, Americans will get the message that parents, the people-raisers, need support and education. Already, the sale of parenting books, the popularity of parenting courses, the demands for day-care and parent participation in the schools show a beginning of a parent-power movement. Consciousness is being raised; the importance of parental influence is being granted. Family influence is seen either as stronger than the schools' efforts or as a bulwark against schools, TV, or peers. Either way, we want parenting to be good and effective. It doesn't matter so much whether family ties are kept up throughout life as in the rural households of old (we still think we can handle retirement, old age, and dying!), but the early parent-child interaction is seen as so crucial that it is worth social investment.

Optimistically, I foresee parent education becoming a part of every curriculum, community organization, and church, complete with apprenticeship programs in which young people could go into families or work with children in group settings. The first experimental programs in parent education have already begun.[19] Besides principles of nutrition, health care, medicine, and management, such programs should include knowledge of child development and the emotional and cognitive needs of children. It is ironic that in our society today we must pass a test and show skill to receive a driving license but nothing is required of future parents. Surely manipulating a car around the roads is a minor responsibility with less social impact and consequences compared to the responsibility of parenting. I do not think we will ever curtail the rights of persons to become parents (too dangerous to our freedom); but I do think we will decide that it is too dangerous not to require some preparation from those embarking upon child rearing. Differences in philosophy, religion, and values could be handled by pluralistic programs in parenting. As the valuation of the child increases and respect for the responsibility of parenting grows, there should be more and more support for parents while they are engaged in the art.

Perhaps my optimism about the future is a reaction to pres-

[19] Janet S. Brown, "Improving Family Life: Action and Reaction," *Journal of Marriage and the Family* (November 1970), pp. 598–609.

ent depression. The state of parenting in the United States can only go up. We seem to specialize in penalizing parents economically, professionally, socially, and with psychic stress. To begin with, they bear the total economic burden of child care, including medical and educational costs. If parents cannot come up with money, then their children starve, remain ill, suffer cold, and stay confined to the narrow world of poverty. Not only do the children suffer and risk being stunted in every way, but parents suffer great anxiety, distress, and guilt over their helplessness to provide for their children. It is suffering twice over; parental despair is the worst burden of poverty.

Yet even parents who are not in severe economic distress are worried. Many cannot depend upon anyone in case of death or illness. If they do not live near their families, or their kinship ties have been broken, they have little social support in parenting. The isolation of many suburban or city families when children are young is debilitating. Public places do not, by and large, welcome children. Children are not invited to social occasions and baby-sitters are rare and expensive. Parents can find themselves in the odd situation in which they are too much with their children at some times and yet not really participating enough in their lives.

Working parents find that there is no allowance made for family duties and they are expected to compete with childless workers. The pressures of work are so stringent that it is hard to give time to family life. Middle-class men particularly suffer parental castration. When there is time off, there may be few parent-child activities available. Children's activities such as the schools, sports, etc., are also set up so that parents are excluded. Each individual in American society moves in solitary unconnected orbit, independent, isolated, on his own in a competitive age-graded group. Those who are connected to "dependents" are hampered and burdened in the race and often excluded in leisure. Today parents are left alone with their burden.

There is not even the status and respect which used to accompany parenthood. A "swinging singles" ideal of freedom and self-realization often takes precedence over family ideals.[20] A non-commitment to children has reached the popular culture through imagery and media. In a healthy reaction to togetherness and the rush to obsessively coupled domestic scenes, the pendulum has swung too far in the other direction. The pressure of anti-child sentiments weighs heavily in some circles. Children are noisy, unpredictable, and demanding; they challenge the existing adult order of cleanliness, property rights, and propriety. The child is the newcomer, the last immigrant; no children allowed. Parents in America are often on the defensive and the target of much hostility and little encouragement. One of the nastier by-products of the population-control movement has been the release of aggression and accusation against parents and children. Why should we support schools with our taxes, etc.? Bias against families and children makes child rearing all the more difficult. A defensive feeling and cutting criticism from others constrict the atmosphere and undermine parental morale. When the birth rate plummets as it has been doing, we want it to be in response to the special privilege and responsibility of parenthood and the needs of all, not in a rejection of a commitment to children. Individualistic, self-centered hedonism never serves a culture well.

So I predict that the pro-child, pro-parenting strains in the culture will have a resurgence, but with more sophisticated realism. The changes in American life have to be faced. Norman Rockwell is a liar in the service of nostalgia. The whole community has to give the support to parents that an extended-

[20] Ellen Peck, *The Baby Trap* (New York: Bernard Geis Associates, 1971); Rita Kramer, "The No-child Family," *The New York Times Magazine* (December 24, 1972), pp. 28–31.

family system once did. Fragile child-care structures must be strengthened and our lip service to child-centered commitments given concrete form. Since we are behind most of the developed countries of the world in our methods of social support, we have much to do. A brief obvious outline can sketch our inadequacies.

Besides parental education there has to be some commitment to a minimum standard of living and health. No more hunger and malnutrition which stunt brain potential. No more lead poisoning. No more shocking infant-mortality rate from inadequate maternal care and prenatal neglect. Other countries have devised systems of public health which remedy gross distortions of human life and so can we. Future parenthood need not, or should not, have to bear subsistence anxieties or conditions damaging to health. Whatever it takes, we do. Birth insurance, infant social security, family allowances, income by right, children's rights—call it what we will but get basic minimum support to parents and children.

Children with special problems need special benefits, or else their parents and siblings are cruelly overburdened. Hardly any single family of an exceptional child can bear the expense of costly medical care or special education or residential care. We provide public schooling for the majority of children, we should provide special programs for the special child. Their parents also need special counseling and help to deal with the extra difficult challenge. Future parents should not fear the total abandonment that can befall parents today whose child needs exceptional care.

Unexceptional needs are just as pressing, such as a network of family centers and day-care programs. When a young family does not have kinship ties, or nearby friends, they are bereft of aid, advice, and the mutual support of others. Never before in man's long history on earth have so many parents been so isolated from social support. Even on our early frontier, isolated neighbors gave each other the help that would have been forthcoming from kinfolk or tribe in earlier eras. Perhaps the struggle against the elements and the small numbers involved (all newcomers) forced people together for mutual aid. But in the cities or suburbs today, the struggle is psychological as well as material, and large numbers of anonymous transients make neighborliness more difficult. Without tribe, kin, or neighbors ready made, we must invent parent-support systems.

A good beginning could be made by directing public status and appreciation to parents. Other countries give their mothers heroine medals, etc., but here we might give tax credits or pensions or some system of recognition much like the veterans' program. Women who have devoted their energies to parenting, particularly need recognition. They could be given status as well as aids in retraining when early parenting is over. A G.I. bill for returning women's education would be a just solution. Today women veterans of intense years of child care get no medals and are often penalized when they try to go back to school or become re-employed. Their years of service and parenting skills are given no social reward and little validation. The most difficult of all human activity is given the least honor. Success in parenting, like one's spiritual condition, has heretofore awaited recognition at the last judgment. That's too long to wait. Parenting and child-rearing skills should be recognized, rewarded, and emulated for the sake of our collective future. A cursory look at the childhoods of every assassin, dictator, and criminal in the jails should convince.

Already the goal of every social agency is to get every child (or adult) out of an institution into a home with foster parents, or a foster parent. An intentional family with therapeutic social parenting can substitute to a greater or lesser extent for biological-social ties. Substitute social parenting needs to be a recognized vocation. So-called professional parents can be arranged for and properly compensated. Foster parenting and foster grandparenting should be encouraged and rewarded. If doctors, therapists, and ministers get pay for their care of a person's needs, why not parents? If all parents were socially rewarded to some extent, there would not be any stigma to social parenting for payment. Child care would be as much esteemed as those professions devoted to repairing the ill effects of distorted child rearing. Some recognition and reward system is needed for future parenting.

Another important support for future parenting and family life involves instituting day-care systems. Having day care available in family centers would be a service to parents and children. Setting up day-care substitutes socially for the extended family, social networks, and larger households of earlier family life. Parents need other adults to help them in caring for their children, and children need other adults and age-mates for optimal growing up. Children used to have a social circle in the busy home-work centers, but now that the work scene has shifted from home to office and factory, women cannot work and care for their children at the same time. Since women work from necessity, choice, and a sense of duty to their vocation, they need facilitating child-care arrangements.[21] Child-care arrangements at work are excellent, for then the child and working parents can interact during the day. Part-time work schedules and neighborhood day-care centers also help working parents, combining family and employment.

Since an infant or small child needs constant care and attachment to one or two or three stable, loving specific caretakers, day-care arrangements in the future will have to be subtly and carefully constructed.[22] Emotions, committed caring, and parent-child bonds must be preserved in a child-

[21] Sidney Callahan, *The Working Mother* (New York: The Macmillan Co., 1971).
[22] Margaret O'Brien Stenfels, *Daycare in the U.S.A.* (New York: Simon & Schuster, 1973).

oriented environment.[23] Perhaps many mothers or fathers will be subsidized to stay home and care for their children with some form of parenting-study leave. The school systems which are already granting the first male paternity leaves are taking a step in this direction. Or child-care workers will be available to come into private homes, or two or three homes banded together. It is important to keep continuity in caretakers and provide stimulating childproof environments. The most important thing, however, is that parents and children become attached in a specific emotional bonding and that parents have enough power to protect their children. If we could have more partner families who live in group arrangements and share the child care, then we can duplicate the support system that most mothers and fathers have traditionally had from their biological family.

But parenthood remains specific and the main work of socialization lies with irreversibly committed long-term parents. Only in naïve theory can one talk of the advantages of "a serene and stable socializer" who is separated from the biological reproducers. In real life socialization is dependent upon emotional involvement. The learning involved in socialization is not all cognitive but dependent upon deep attachments which facilitate identification and imitation. Children model themselves on many people that they admire in the course of growing up; but it's the emotional involvement which facilitates learning and imitation. Attention is focused upon the person who provides pleasure, security, comfort, and reward. We attend what we like. Closeness, clinging, and attachment facilitate the mutual interaction which stimulates learning and memory. As we said earlier, intellectual and emotional development is all bound up together in the human young.

A case can be made for the unserene socializer. If a parent

23 Gilbert Y. Steiner, "Day Care Centers: Hype or Hope?" *Trans-Action* (July–August 1971), pp. 50–57.

cannot be excited, delighted, and anxious about his child, does he care enough? I doubt it. If all outcomes are equal, or all children interchangeable, the emotional investment is tepid indeed. There is such a thing in parenting as "pathologic composure" or absence of reaction.[24] The emotional temperature has got to be higher to maintain the proper level of caressing, caring, and constant interaction that stimulates a child's development. I think parenthood is specific in human beings, just as it is in the mother-child relationship of monkeys. Even mother monkeys know their own. Security, comfort, and nurture are provided in a one-to-one specific and highly possessive relationship.

Human beings are heirs to an even more intensified parental involvement, and fathers can participate equally. In human parenthood, fathers and non-biological adopted parents can assume and enlarge the bonds of mother-child ties, but the specific preferences and possessiveness remain. Efforts to erase the possessive components of parenting have rarely been successful. In the kibbutz experiments, for instance, the important role of specific parents was never suppressed and over the years has steadily grown.[25] Today, in many kibbutzim the parental living quarters have expanded and the children are not only visited and put to bed by their own parents as in the past, but also sleep with their parents away from the children's house.

Indeed, the kibbutz is an interesting case of reinventing parents, along with reinventing the clan or extended family. All of the kibbutz members feel a tie to "their" children and are involved in their upbringing, even to taking turns in their care. The specific parents have always had their specific private

[24] Henry, *op. cit.*, p. 35.
[25] *Children in Collectives*, Peter B. Neubauer, ed. (Springfield, Ill.: Charles C. Thomas, 1965); Albert I. Rabin, *Growing Up in the Kibbutz* (New York: Springer Pub., 1965).

time each day, in addition to nursing in infancy, and occasional daytime visits. But a reinvention of parents comes with the system of assigning child-care workers to the children's groups. A female caretaker is assigned to a few children when they are very young, but at school age there is a male teacher and female housekeeper for each group. This caretaker and teacher are in essence parallel and substitute parents during the day when the biological parents are working nearby. With so much parenting and adult involvement it is no wonder that the kibbutz children show no juvenile delinquency, homosexuality, and few other grave signs of detachment and social deviance.

But even in the kibbutz, bad parent-child relationships can cause disturbance in the child.[26] While no natural or biological parent can thoroughly destroy a child in such a system of checks and balances, group supervision, and communal care, still rejecting or neurotic parents in bad marriages can pass on their troubles to their children. (In two hours a day yet!) While the parent-child tie may be less exclusive and intense than in usual Western-style nuclear families, it is still potent. The important point to be made is that much parallel, complementary or concomitant parenting can be provided by an affiliated group without destroying the parent-child bonds. A child can become deeply attached to several continuous caretakers and get the specific loving interaction it needs. Even those who maintain that a child forms a primary attachment to one and only one parental figure still think it possible to have complementary caretaking without destroying the bond's intensity.

In the future, parents in the United States will seek complementary and parallel parenting for their young children. As long as parents can be in control of the care (more than in the kibbutz or communist systems) and it can be individualized

26 Bruno Bettelheim, *The Children of the Dream* (New York: The Macmillan Co., 1969).

for them and the needs of their children, no harm will be done. A state-imposed regime à la China and Russia with standardized programs including political indoctrination could never be accepted by those committed to pluralism and diversity. Indeed, in affluent America there will always be a majority who will avoid all communal care in favor of private individual home care. The growing movement against public schools and toward more individualized and decentralized education would be even stronger in the case of infants and young children.

Pluralistic solutions to parenting needs will also become more frequent in the future. I foresee more partner-families who share co-operative consumer needs and child-rearing arrangements. More and more communes will be created. Many more young parents will unite to share their resources in ways that will remind us of the earlier extended family or frontier households. Children will be cared for by "aunts" and "uncles," with "cousins" who will not be blood relations but intentional families or fictive kin. The children will benefit from the added security and breadth of more adult involvement. When twins have married twins, or brothers married sisters, and lived in close proximity, the double marriages have been particularly strong and successful. Perhaps this bonding of two pairs could be a viable and supportive arrangement to be imitated. While few people can find a whole group they can happily co-operate with, another pair of trusted friends is possible.

Since fewer people will have big families in the future, increased joining together will give children the experience with siblings that they need. The mutual child care of two sets of parents who can spell each other off, or come to one another's aid in an emergency, is also important. I am sure that a completely communal lifestyle would never be satisfactory to most American parents and families, but some adjoining arrangements could increase in popularity. Two-family houses, adjoining apartments, condominiums with common rooms—we'll see ever more experiments which succeed in combining privacy with common living. Parents may be finally learning the lesson that in solidarity there is strength.

Ironically, parents can often communicate with their children better when they do so in a context which includes other adults and children. The stimulus of other people of varying ages and other dialogues makes the parent-child dialogue less constrained and self-conscious. Give and take becomes easier when there are more players and the sides can keep changing. Everyone in a family is more stimulated and less lonesome when there are peers to talk with for support, and domestic maintenance chores are lightened by company. Working together lightens the load. The tremendous amount of physical work and supervision in parenting can be done more easily in common.

But perhaps the psychic burdens of parenting would be most helped by communal co-operation. Just to have caring, involved fellow parents to talk with is a great help. There are many decisions to be made in the course of parenting and few people who know or care about the specific family situation. In a pluralistic situation without a common cultural consensus, individuals need more time devoted to constructing socially a common reality. Parents keep their perspective on values through common cause and conversation. What's really important? And what's the best way to get to our goals? I foresee a growing parental movement, even when co-operative living would not be chosen.

In sum, I see future parenthood becoming a more self-conscious process which is taken more seriously both by parents and everybody else in the society. The response will be a widening and deepening of the parental task to include collective solutions in day-care arrangements, co-operative living, and new forms of parent solidarity. In an optimistic view of the future, one sees the isolated, competitive individualistic model of American parenthood transformed into a more co-operative communal model, with a greater parental concern diffused in the population. In the best of futures, parenting will not be solely an isolated, anxious enterprise. Fewer people may choose to parent, but when they do, they and their children will not be abandoned by the rest of the society. Forms of communal support will be worked out which do not impose the uniform solutions of state socialism. Ideally, parents should possess enough control to protect and nurture their children, but not so much that the children are reduced to products which must suit to survive. Both parent and child need room to move so that they can be fully human and rightfully relate to one another.

Our growing understanding of the complexity of human consciousness will make us in the future cherish our specific human development of parent-child bonds. Of course, plasticity, change, and technology are our human specialties, but so are emotion and affect. Feelings and loving commitments keep us going as a surviving species which must socialize each generation anew. For the future, we guard the delicate balance of forces which keep us caring for each other, nurturing the parental dimension in our individual and collective selves. Only human beings beget humans.

Epilogue

Having written so many words emphasizing the importance of emotion in parent-child bonding, I find I have expressed precious few of my own. (But there's no dearth of opinion and value judgments.) Most assuredly, I do not write about parenting from a detached and confident viewpoint. I write in the midst of middle parenting, where passions have not cooled and perspectives have not been put into proper proportion with the passing of time. I am struggling to be a good parent along with everyone else and I have no magic secret of success. We have our ups and downs like everybody and who knows how the story will turn out in the end?

I do know, however, as surely as I know anything, that nothing, but nothing, has ever been more of a personal challenge than parenting. Rearing a child is to be searched and known, to meet life in depth. The strong emotions which sweep through the parenting processes are unbelievable to others. It's hard to describe the peak experiences of joy, the crushing depths of despair, the anger, the resentment, contentment, and quiet happiness. How understandable that parents and children murder each other, or sacrifice themselves for the other's well-being.

All the ambivalence of human nature is displayed in family life. A whole range of responses are found in the intimacy of the parent-child relationship—including apathy and indifference. Boredom and numbness also frequently appear and produce their own anxieties. Some cruelties and quarrels seem mostly an effort to feel again and get in touch with one another. Personal styles differ so drastically that all happy and unhappy families differ in their own way. But there's an interfamily resemblance, for good reason. In the parent-child relationship, as I've tried to show in the preceding chapters, we get our notion of what being a human being is all about. Cognitive styles, coping styles, and emotional styles are catching. Even physical displays or appearances tend toward symmetry—all the way down to the family dog.

But I would hardly be the child of my parents if I did not believe in the possibilities of positive change with effort, will, and reasoned insight. My generation of American parents will only add that the sociocultural influences in the general population are also powerful. Outside forces are real; there are things beyond the control of the most perfect parents. War, disease, public assassinations, accidents, social breakdown revealed in drug epidemics, unemployment, and riots—all the troubles of troubled times and external events can become entwined in private troubles and private parent-child dramas. There is no wheel of fortune turning inexorably, as the Elizabethans thought, but there are complexities, coincidences, and the unforeseen interaction of multiple factors which keep us from controlling our fate.

Parents trying to effect a successful protective buffering process cannot always do so. When a nursing mother's milk can contain radiation from atomic weapons, private parental protection is threatened. Perhaps the greatest pain in parenting arises when one is helpless to protect because of forces beyond one's control. To be unable to help your child provokes a special suffering. Shrinking from such vulnerability, many people refuse to parent; like John Kennedy they see children as "our hostages to fortune." Others hesitate in fear, doubting their ability to be a good parent.

Once into parenting, who among us can help but experience self-doubts? But surely this uncertainty can be a creative force, urging parents to try harder and think more deeply about their values. There's even a place for good guilt which can honestly recognize failings and lead to improvement as person and parent. Parental guilt only gets out of hand when wallowing in guilt hinders present efforts to live well. We should all remember that the perfect parent has never lived. Moreover, if it's any comfort, some of the greatest people of all time appear to have failed as parents. Personal development and success are not the same as inducing a child "to increase in wisdom and stature, and in favor with God and man."

Unknown and hidden aspects of life are brought close in the personal experience of parenthood. We cannot judge any case with surety because there are too many factors at work in each person's development. Parent-child relationships are affected by too many variables. Who knows how much to weigh parenting along with the influence of genetic factors, temperament, family size, position in the family, sex, socioeconomic conditions, race, region, peers, schooling, other adult models, the media, and finally, random chance events. Parents either tend to take credit for the good and blame the bad on outside forces, or vice versa. But cause and effect are never simple or clear-cut in parent-child interactions.

Our knowledge is still too incomplete for explanations. It's far more appropriate for parents and others to be grateful when things go well in parenting; hope continuously, and without judging, supports parents in their sorrows and disappointments. Meanwhile, parents keep on striving for more wisdom. Our humanization as a species has been founded on the parental enterprise, so why stop now? We may dispute the relative influences of parenting, or debate the goals, rights, and cultural values which parents should have, or argue the most effective methods of child rearing. But no one doubts the crucial importance of parenting to children. For the sake of children, we take parenting seriously and try to improve.